THE BLACK
DONNELLYS

THE BLACK DONNELLYS

THOMAS P. KELLEY

FIREFLY BOOKS LTD.

A FIREFLY BOOK

Copyright © 1993 Samuel Roy Enterprises

Canadian Cataloguing in Publication Data
Kelley, Thomas P., 1908-
    The Black Donnellys

ISBN 1-895565-24-3

1. Donnelly family.   2. Murder — Ontario — Lucan.
3. Criminals — Ontario — Lucan.   1. Title
HV6810.L8K44 1993   364.1'523'0922   C93-093218-8

First published in 1954.
This edition published in 1993.

Published by:
Firefly Books Ltd.
250 Sparks Ave.
Willowdale, Ontario, Canada
M2H 2S4

Published in the U.S. by:
Firefly Books (U.S.) Inc.
P.O. Box 1338
Ellicott Station
Buffalo, NY
14205

Cover design by Sheila McGraw

Printed in Canada

CONTENTS

INTRODUCTION

The True Story of Canada's Most Barbaric Feud

"So hurry to your homes, good folks,
Lock doors and windows tight.
And pray for dawn, The Black Donnellys
Will be abroad tonight."

— Old Song

The letter, sent from Port Huron, Michigan, adressed to William Donnelly of Lucan, Ontario, and dated February 14, 1880, read:

"William Donnelly: You and your surviving relatives have long been a disgrace to the Lucan district. Heed some good advice while the breath of life is still in you. You and your remaining brothers get to hell out of the country while there is still time, or you will get the same as your parents and the others did."

It was signed: "One who had the pleasure of helping to kill your mother and father, and saw your brothers fall."

It seems that the Donnellys of Lucan were none too popular. Of their slayers it was said: "The men that killed the Donnellys deserve special seats in heaven."

The terrible Donnelly feud, by far the most notorious and violent in the annals of Canada, was an almost endless series of depredations with human depravity at its worst.

The feud began in the spring of 1847, and only a few hours after James Donnelly, an Irish immigrant, first arrived in Lucan from his native Tipperary. It lasted nearly thirty-three years; was marked with murders, gang wars, highway robbery, mass arson, derailed trains, mutilations and barbarisms paralleling the Dark Ages.

For sheer savagery, the notorious Hatfield-McCoy affair or the lawless exploits of Jesse James, were as a Victorian tea-party compared to the Donnelly feud.

Not that such a record of past violence should come as a surprise, Canada's history of crime and criminals is by no means as placid as many believe. For much more than a century, Canada has had criminals as ruthless and crimes as macabre as you will find anywhere in the world. But there was only one Donnelly feud. Fortunately, for the Dominion, it stands alone.

It was during the feud that Lucan (formerly Marysville) became known as "the wildest spot in Canada," as its night skies glared with the flames from burning structures and masked riders thundered down lonely sideroads with shouts of triumph. Vandalism in full swing, street brawls were numerous as were gun battles with law officers, while crops were destroyed, coaches waylaid, horses mutilated and poisoned cattle left dying in the fields. Outsiders avoided the district as one would a plague-stricken area.

Then it all ended, suddenly and unexpectedly. The Donnelly feud was finally climaxed in a drastic manner akin to its lengthy duration; the massacre of an entire household during the dark hours before the dawn of February 4, 1880.

At the time, the massacre and the trials that followed received national attention, being featured for weeks in the Dominion's leading newspapers. It is doubtful if the most secluded hamlets throughout the nation were not aware of at least some of the happenings of "The Biddulph Township Tragedy."

Though more than three score and ten years have passed since that final night of murder, strange stories are still told out on the Roman Line, the long road that runs by the Donnelly farmhouse, and on which many of the outrages occured. On stormy nights when the elders gather around the kitchen lamp, while the wind sweeps over broad fields and snowdrifts pile high to the windows, you will hear grim tales of the Donnellys.

I know, for I have heard them.

You will hear how old Johannah Donnelly cursed those who were killing her husband and family, even as life was being clubbed from her, and how every member of the mob, in the last raid on the Donnelly farmhouse died a violent death. You will be told that on certain nights as dirty clouds drift across the moon, phantom forms on phantom horses can be seen hurrying along the Roman Line. "The restless spirits of the Donnellys still seeking vengeance," is the explanation. There will be tales of past terror and lawlessness almost beyond belief; and you will be sure to hear that foremost story — that even now it is impossible to get a horse to go past the old Donnelly place after midnight.

Shortly after the turn of the century, some backroads bard set down the words:

"Birds don't sing and men don't smile,
Out on the Roman Line.
Their faces grim and so they'll be,

Until the end of time.
For the midnight hour brings alarm,
And horses won't pass the Donnelly farm,
Stay off that road or you'll come to harm,
Out on the Roman Line."

The material for the following pages was gathered from old newspapers, police and court records, as well as other unimpeachable sources and by several trips to the Lucan area.

T.P.K.

Toronto
April, 1953

CHAPTER ONE

Jim Donnelly Came to Lucan —

Jim Donnelly came to Lucan,
And trouble soon did start.
The devil was in Donnelly's eyes,
Murder was in his heart.

— Old Song

There was the right amount of sunshine and the right amount of breeze. Even the old-timers around London, Ontario, were as one — for once — in admitting it was a "grand day for a hangin." The day was June 5, 1832.

Like other executions, the hanging of Jonathan Sovereen was an event long looked forward to; a welcomed excitement in the humdrum and laborious lives of Canada's pioneer farmers. Lunch baskets had been filled the previous evening, homespun 'bests' put in order. Farm wives looked forward to meeting old friends, while their men discussed crops and made frequent sojourns to nearby bars. For the youngsters there would be new scenes, new faces, and always the hopes of obtaining some of the enormous peppermint "Bull's Eyes" (three for a cent) prominently displayed on most store counters.

In brief, it promised to be a gala occasion for all — except the condemned man.

1

Long before the dawn of June 5, carriages and wagons began to rumble into London, making for the corners of Dundas and Ridout Streets, the designated site for the execution. Streaming from all sections of the city, its inhabitants added to the ranks. By 10 a.m. there was an estimated crowd of six thousand, noisy and impatient. Adjoining bars did a land office business; the contents of lunch baskets steadily diminished.

Conversations of the crowd were general. There was comment on the recent hanging of one Cornelius Burleigh, and the violent manner of his kicks and contortions as he slowly strangled to death. Trap door drops were not in vogue. Burleigh's case was discussed to some length. Nothing squeamish about the hardy Irish and Scotch immigrants, who comprised most of the first settlers of London's Middlesex County and battled its wilderness. They couldn't afford to be.

Around 11 a.m., the appearance of several officials and constables on the roof of the two-storey building that was Lawrason and Goodhue's store, announced the awaited execution. Then came the condemned Jonathan Sovereen, brawny, red-bearded — and smiling!

Fear had certainly not claimed Jonathan. At the edge of the roof he bowed, greeted the spectators with a loud, "Just call me Johnnie," and despite his bound arms sprightly danced the jig that brought cheers from the crowd and did not surprise those who knew him. It seems that in his own rural district Jonathan Sovereen was a prankster of note; a forerunner of the loaded cigar type who delighted in frightening the hell out of people.

There were at least a dozen known occasions when he rose up before a lighted farmhouse window, late at night, a white sheet over his head as he gave out with ominous moans. He'd howl with laughter at the panic of those within. He had devised and used several crude forms of the modern stink bomb; and the very mention of the time he horrified the women at the harvest supper, by removing raisins from a rice pudding and substituting dead flies, still brought stitches to many a rural son. Jonathan Sovereen was a card!

Jonathan was also a mass murderer.

In his spare moments, when not playing the village clown, he had engaged in horse stealing. His wife eventually learning of his nefarious sideline and threatened to expose it. Again, she stood in the way of the love interest he had shifted to a comely Indian maid, whose family had recently settled in the district. So one night, armed with an axe and quietly entering his house, Jonathan had hacked his sleeping wife and their six children to death. This, the law decided, was carrying a joke a bit too far, even for Jonathan. So he wound up his days as central figure for a public hanging.

The execution was marked by a shocking and unexpected highlight.

Pushed from the roof and swung from a beam protruding from the store, the rope broke and the murderer plunged to the ground before his audience. The noose still around his neck and a foot of rope dangling from it, he rose to his feet only to be taken back to the roof for a repeat performance. But Jonathan was gay and undaunted to the end. Again on the roof, he recognized three acquaintances below him, and wagered each a round of drinks that the second rope would likewise snap and he be given his freedom.

Prankster Jonathan Sovereen lost his bet.

The more morbid came forward for a closer inspection, but gradually the crowd broke up. The show was over, there were crops that needed attention. True, to many families the holiday meant hours of extra drudgery for at least a week; but it had given them a year's material for daily conversations and yarns their children could tell future grandchildren. Finally, amid loud farewells and promises to meet at the next execution, wagon wheels started turning homeward, some for many miles. One elderly woman at the Sovereen hanging told of a two days journey she had made from distant Hamilton, "to see the fun."

Among the last to leave the victim were the three men who had accepted Sovereen's wager. One of them recalled it and mentioned something about his bravery.

"Bravery?" came the answer of one with a brogue you could cut with a knife. "The spalpeen and his shenanigans. He knew if he'd live he'd have to buy the drinks; now that he's dead he isn't able to. Arrah the man was a born chate. He knew he couldn't lose!"

Among those who witnessed the hanging of Jonathan Sovereen was one Felix Marra. A few days later, writing to his friend Dan Donnelly, in distant Tipperary, Ireland, Marra referred to the hanging but mainly stressed the opportunities offered in the new world. He urged Donnelly to sell his small farm and migrate to Canada.

Over in Ireland, Dan Donnelly read the letter with a tired smile. Go to Canada? Why not ask him to fly to the moon? At fifty, the work-worn Donnelly looked sixty and felt seventy! With a run-down farm, an ailing wife and three children — up to his neck in debt as well — the future looked anything but promising. Go to Canada, was it? Why he'd be lucky if that old donkey of his would be able to get him to town with the next cartload of vegetables.

But there was one member of his household who didn't think a migration to the New World was so impossible.

His son, sixteen-year old Jim Donnelly, was all for it and said so. A new land that offered adventure, and perhaps some battles with those wild red men he had heard about. The boy's blue eyes were wide.

"When do we start?" he wanted to know.

Dan Donnelly didn't answer at once. He recalled his own youth and boyhood dreams. They had seemed so possible — then. His was a listless tone when he finally replied, "We won't be goin', Jim. That is, neither your mother or I will be goin' to Canada. Too many years on both of us. As for yourself; well maybe, someday —."

"Yes?"

"Someday you may be able to get there, son."

Young Jim Donnelly never forgot the words, though for some time it appeared that he, too, would spend his life in Ireland. The passing years didn't bring riches, but they brought the death of his parents and he continued to work the small farm near Mullinahone. Then in his twenty-fifth year — 1841 — a journey took Jim Donnelly to Clonmel where, under violent circumstances prophetic of the future, he first looked into the eyes of Johannah Foley.

Johannah had been born and lived near the Galty Mountains in southern Tipperary, where her father was a rough-and-tumble fighter of note. Perhaps that's where she got some of her training for the grim years ahead. At the time she met her future spouse Johannah was eighteen, had stern and swarthy features, big hands, broad shoulders and agate-hard eyes. She looked like and should have been a man, her sex undoubtedly robbing the bare-knuckle prize ring of a prospective champion. In later years she sprouted a miniature Vandyke, wore red flannels and told of never having been "much of a beauty." Her picture proves the words to be a gross understatement.

Old records prove Johannah to have been the primary instigator of most of the trouble of the thirty-three year Donnelly feud; they tell she would stress to her seven sons that she could never look upon them with true motherly pride till, like their father, each had killed "at least" one man; and of her falling to her knees, praying their souls would roast in hell if they ever forgave their enemies. A charming old lady, Johannah would smoke her pipe and relate stories of her youth in the Galty Mountains. According to her, the districts must have been so tough the canary birds sang bass.

As for Jim Donnelly, he was an undeniably handsome man. Even his enemies admitted it and The Globe of February 28, 1880, proclaims it. He was not, as some have written, a tall man, being but seven inches over five feet; but he was well-built, unusually muscular and fast-moving, with good features, even white teeth and curly, jet-black hair. Utterly fearless and quickly aroused, Donnelly never forgot an injury, factual or fancied.

The first meeting of Johannah and Jim would hardly have been approved by Emily Post. It was neither under scented boughs, desert stars or beside a woodland stream. There was no balcony climbing nor quoting of, "By yon blessed moon." Instead, fate threw them together under circumstances dear to the heart of both. They met in the thick of a wild and gory shillalah battle.

It seems that Jim Donnelly and ten or so other bold boys from Mullinahone, had journied to the Clonmel Fair for frolic and fight, and the more of the latter the better. There they met a local gang, numerous drinks of poteen followed; then someone said something someone else did not like, and in less than it takes to whistle "The Wearin' Of The Green," shillalahs were swinging, the fight was on and everyone was happy.

Jim Donnelly, a smile on his lips, had rushed into the thick of the fray and was giving a fine account of himself, when his club was torn from his hands. Then he felt a dig in the ribs, wheeled and there was Johannah — with proffered shillalah. Her thoughtfulness aroused the same instant love within him as his fighting spirit did in her. He took the club and resumed combat, but after cracking a few more skulls he turned and thanked the obliging colleen. She smiled, wished him luck, told him to keep up the good work and watched him with admiring eyes.

Evidently the way to Jim Donnelly's heart was with a shillalah; for a short while later the two, in a low-back cart, journeyed to the church and were joined. The following year Johannah gave birth to James Jr. He was destined to be the first of the Donnellys to die.

For three years following the birth of her baby, Johannah, ambitious and tireless, helped her husband by doing a man's work in the fields, the housework as a sideline, and faith and begorrah the two still found time to enjoy the finer things in life by attending every wake, funeral and shillalah brawl in the district, as well as to make plans for the future; the foremost being a migration to Canada. Theirs was an all-out effort and long hours in the fields, along with strict economy, finally paid off.

Donnelly was able to put a bit of money aside which together with the sale of his farm, made his boyhood dreams possible.

There was one event prior to his sailing, however, that was destined for momentous importance in the years to come. On a night in January 1845, as the wind wailed and snowflakes fell heavily — Johannah later said, "The auld woman was pluckin' her geese" — the second son, William, was born. But there was no rejoicing that night in the small farmhouse near Mulinahone. Instead, the parents gazed at the mite in shocked silence. For William, who was to be referred to by the enemies of the Donnellys as "the worst of the whole damn lot," was born with a deformity. A clubfoot.

The following February Jim Donnelly and his family set sail for the New World; their destination, London, Ontario, Canada.

Anyone up on his history of criminals can tell you that Dr. Thomas Neil Cream, the notorious poisoner of the last century, began his private practice and is suspected of having murdered his first victim in London, Ontario. Also that the city is the birthplace of Herbert Emerson Wilson, the one-time minister and king of the cracksmen, who is reputed to have stolen $16,000,000 from various safes throughout America during the roaring twenties. But when Jim Donnelly arrived in London, in 1845, nearly two score years were to pass before Wilson made his debut to the world, and even the cross-eyed Dr. Cream was but a gleam in his daddy's eye.

The land for the present site of London, obtained from the Indians in a treaty dated May 22, 1784, knew the tread of Scottish immigrants before the turn of the nineteenth century. One Ronald McDonald obtained a patent of land in 1798. The Campbells, the McDuffs, McFifes and members of other clans followed. A black settlement arose on the London and Goderich Road in the late 1820's.

Then came the men from the land of the Shamrock. Many of them settled in and around the village of Lucan, in Biddulph Township, seventeen miles to the north of London. They were fearless, hardy men, who had crossed a great ocean in small ships, to make homes for themselves and families, and face the hardships of wilderness life. A bit on the rough side, they were also superstitious and had brought their banshees and leprechauns with them to the New World. Easily aroused and with violent tempers, most of them, however, were loyal and honest; hard workers, hard fighters — and hard drinkers. At one time, though the population was less than five hundred, there were nine bars in Lucan, including Madill's Hotel, The Central Hotel, McRoberts' Old Dominion Hotel, The Dublin House — "Tis many the foin blow that was struck there" — Fitzhenry's Hotel and The Western Bar; the latter famed as the place where Robert Donnelly made his memorable challenge.

In 1879, in a time period of less than thirty days, both Fitzhenry's Hotel and McRoberts' Old Dominion Hotel were destroyed by fire. The cause? According to the surrounding countryside there was only one: "The work of the Black Donnellys! Up to their old tricks again!"

Biddulph Township was organized in January 1842, with Thomas Courcey, Clerk, and James Hodgins, District Councillor. Among the first inhabitants of Biddulph were — and get a load of these names — the Thadeus Twohys, the Uriah Monaghans, the Michael O'Timothy Sullivans, the Darby O'Kelly O'Tooles; Patrick Ryan, Michael Daniel O'Brian and Jeremiah Kilgallan Malone. The Mulligans, Lannigans, Hannigans, Flannigans, Mannigans and Brannigans; the Kelleys, the Sweeneys, the Heenans, the Harrigans, the Duffys, the Shannons, the Keenans and Feenans. The O'Maras, O'Haras, O'Donnels, O'Connels, O'Donnahues, O'Hogans, O'Garritys, O'Flaritys, Mahones and O'Mahones. And by special permission of the copyright owner, one Daniel O'Shaughnessy Patrick Mulcahey. Needless to say, all any would-be suicide had to do was to go up to Biddulph and shout, "To hell with St. Patrick!"

A church was erected in 1849, on the site of where the present one now stands. The first pastor was the Rev. Thadeus Kerwan.

On arriving in London, Donnelly got in touch with Felix Marra, who had written the letter to his father thirteen years earlier, and had prospered. Marra secured the teamster job Jim Donnelly held for two years; but Johannah felt that London "crowded her in;" she yearned for a farmhouse and wide fields, and reminded her spouse of the Government Land Grants. She suggested the Lucan district. "We belong on a farm, Jim. The boys will be growing up and need lots of room." At the time, Johannah was again pregnant.

After the two finally decided on a return to the rural life, most of the Donnelly capital was spent on a team of horses, a stout wagon and two cows. The family possessions were piled on the wagon, the two tethered cows trailed behind; and on a May day in the year 1847 the horses were headed towards Lucan and Biddulph Township. Around sundown the Donnelly wagon pulled up near a sideroad, a short distance outside the village.

In later years Johannah recalled, "The little birds were singin' fit to split their throats."

Camp was made, supper served and the two youngsters put to bed, while the gathering dusk gave way to darkness and stars began to appear. Originally intending to wait till the following day before entering Lucan, it was at last agreed that a more ethical course would be for Jim to stroll into the village, give the place the once-over and perhaps meet some future neighbors. Johannah suggested he take a club along with him. Nothing like a good first impression on prospective neighbors.

Donnelly declined the club with a soft, "Tis needless, Aroon;" but as he drew near the village he slipped a fist-sized rock into his coat-pocket, just in case, then went forward to mingle with society.

His first stop was — naturally — the first saloon. Before it was the wooden sidewalk, a long hitching-rail and saddled horses of pioneer farmers, then the muddy street. From within came the gleam of lights, loud laughs and boisterous voices. After long and laborious hours, hardy sons of the sod were having their fun. Donnelly entered, pushed his way to the bar, motioned to a bottle and was served a stiff one. Downing it, he was wiping his lips with the back of his hand when he noticed the steady gaze of the one next to him. He returned the stare, eyes met and held a minute then Jim Donnelly pushed his glass back on the bar and spoke his first words in the village of Lucan:

"What the hell are you lookin' at, you horse-faced bastard?"

CHAPTER TWO

The Murder of John Farrell

Donnelly 'squatted' on John Farrell's land,
Just laughed when asked to pay.
Then with iron bar struck Farrell dead,
At a logging bee one day.
                                        — Old Song

Jim Donnelly's first night in the village of Lucan was a howling social success; a memorable occasion. There were numerous drinks, many angry words and threats, and to top it off he had and easily won two fist fights. Neither fight lasted long; a roundhouse right laid out the man at the bar with the inquisitive stare in jig-time. Later a friend of the fallen gladiator tried to avenge him. Woeful failure marked the effort. And just to make the night complete, on his way back to his wife Donnelly lifted half-a-dozen roosting biddies from a henhouse. He was never one to seek popularity.

Returning to the wagon, Donnelly related the events of the night to Johannah. Her bosom swelled with pride. The following morning the two set out to find a family home-site.

Canada is a vast land of over three million six hundred thousand square miles, and Government Grants, in 1847, were easily obtained. Yet with almost the entire Dominion to choose from, Donnelly settled on privately owned land, a hundred acres some four miles from Lucan — Lot 18 on the 6th Concession of Biddulph Township. Biddulph, bounded on the west and north by Huron County, on the east by Perth County, was and is a flat, fertile district, ideal for farming. Donnelly saw a good future; the fact he had "squatted" on the land of another failed to worry him. To his way of thinking, possession was nine-tenths of the law.

The owner of the property had no such broadminded views. A few days later, on hearing of the presence of the trespasser, he rode over to his property to tell Donnelly there had been a mistake. Jim Donnelly, busy felling trees for a log cabin and handling his axe as though it were a hatchet, implied that if any mistakes were being made, the owner was making them by opening his big mouth. The latter looked into the newcomer's eyes and saw the devil.

Then Johannah barged forward, her hands curled into fists. She glared hard at the landowner and wanted to know if he was looking for trouble. "We've plenty of it," she informed "and tis a foin mornin' for a fight."

"But — but —" sputtered the other.

Donnelly still held his axe. His eyes narrowed. "Mister," he spoke with a sinister calm, "you just better forget all about this land, turn that horse around and ride out of here while you're able to. I'll overlook your mistake this time."

"My — my mistake?" exclaimed the rightful owner. "You say you'll overlook my mistake?" He gazed around in a helpless daze.

Donnelly began to swing the axe in a suggestive manner. "But don't let it happen again and I wouldn't come back here if I were you. I might not be so polite. Now get goin'!"

The landowner did just that and, incredible as it may seem, never made any legal attempt to regain his property. He seemed content to get off it with his life. "When that Donnelly glares at you, you seem to hear the sound of shovels digging your grave," he told when relating the story that night and on succeeding nights in the Lucan bars. He aroused great indignation; the general advice was to throw the intruder off the land, but offers to help were conspicuous by their absence. Donnelly stayed on the land and finished his cabin, unassisted by any neighboring homeraising bee. Johannah, as good as any man in lifting a log, even though she was pregnant, was his only help.

His home completed, Jim Donnelly was ready to start breaking ground. For this he needed a plough, stump pullers and other necessary farm implements. Just how he got them all is still a matter of speculation, for it is known he had little money when he arrived in Lucan. "Now I'm not saying he stole them," an elderly Lucanite told the writer. "But when I was a young boy, I remember my father telling me that farming equipment, strangely disappearing at night from the barns of surrounding farmers, somehow always had the damnedest habit of turning up at the Donnelly place." Well, at least it was an obliging habit — for Jim Donnelly.

Four months after settling on the land, on September 16, 1847, Johannah gave birth to her third son, John. John was destined to end his days, sprawled face forward in a February snow, "with so many shots in his body he would have had to be cut to mincemeat to get them all out."

During the following eight years, Jim Donnelly whipped the wilderness to a standstill and created a rich, self-sufficient farm. Johannah, on her part, presented him with four more sons, named in order of birth, Patrick,

Michael, Robert and Thomas. Johannah's last child was a daughter, Jennie. She was to be known as the belle of the district. The mother was as fiercely protective of her children as a she-wolf with cubs.

The first eight years of Jim Donnelly's residence in Biddulph Township were marked only with petty quarrels and accusations between him and his neighbors; but his name gradually became an unpopular one. "The Black Donnelly's" moniker was to come later. Of course on nearly every Saturday night Donnelly rode into Lucan for a drop of spirits at one of its bars, and there were the occasional fist fights with one of its citizens. Johannah agreed with her husband that a man needs a certain amount of relaxation. At the bars, Donnelly usually had to drink alone and was inevitably the object of hostile gazes. Those around him had not forgotten how he obtained his land; again, the name Donnelly was now connected with nearly every petty theft that occurred in the district.

Then in 1855 John Farrell came into the picture and dark clouds began to gather, with murder in the offing.

Farrell was a direct antithesis to the timid landowner who had been ordered off his own place by Donnelly. John Farrell was a big, unkempt Irishman, with a neck the size of a stovepipe and just as dirty, who would fight at the drop of a hat, drink at the pop of a cork, and had a reputation for both in his own district. A one-time blacksmith, he came from nearby Perth County, had a little money and had been told that the property Donnelly settled on could be bought "dirt-cheap." He interviewed the landowner who warned of the danger of trying to get Donnelly off the place.

Farrell's smile was grim; he had always welcomed trouble. "Let me worry about that," was his answer.

"Once the place is mine, I'll get Donnelly off it — and in a hell of a hurry, too!"

For some time Farrell had been hearing stories of the quarrelsome squatter from Tipperary, and had told that the day would come when he would 'put the thieving blackguard in his place.' Within an hour after becoming the new owner of the farm, Farrell, accompanied by a friend, was on a horse and galloping towards it. It was late afternoon when the two pulled up before the log cabin that had been built by Jim Donnelly. Several of his small sons were playing in the front yard, including ten-year old, club-footed William; the surrounding fields showed their crops of corn, wheat and barley.

Jim Donnelly appeared from the barn and came forward as the two men dismounted at the front gate and walked through it. Farrell came directly to the point. "You're Donnelly, of course, and my name is Farrell. I've got news for you, this place is mine; I've just bought it and I'm giving you exactly one hour to get off it. Sixty minutes by the watch."

For several seconds Jim Donnelly stared at the other; it seemed to take him that long to grasp the words. Then a slow smile came to his lips before he gave a mocking laugh. Donnelly was a good five inches shorter and forty pounds lighter than Farrell, but he answered with, "And suppose I don't want to get off?"

"Then I'll throw you off and give you a sore tail in the bargain," was the informative reply. Donnelly laughed again and Farrell added, his voice rising with his temper. "And any of your lip and I'll do it right now."

Jim Donnelly nodded in a satisfied manner. He took off the coat he was wearing, tossed it on the ground and replied, "Shuren you're a man after my own kidney, and I'll be pleased to oblige you." His eyes went to his children. "Now boys, watch your father and learn." Then to Farrell, "Just put up your fists, Mister, and we'll get started." The small sons of Jim Donnelly shouted approval of their sire's words, and sat back to watch the battle and cheer for him.

Farrell's eyes widened. He had not expected his challenge to be so readily and joyfully accepted. Not that he was afraid; John Farrell didn't know the meaning of the word fear; he had proved that in the past. But the utter indifference of the other man puzzled him. Farrell's gaze went to his friend. The latter, thinking his services were wanted, started to come forward when all of them heard, "Another step, Mister, will be your last!"

It was Johannah, standing in the cabin doorway, eyes narrowed, swarthy features scowling and hands pointing the family musket at Farrell's friend. She admitted, "I'm not much of a shot," then warned, "but even if I do miss you I can always bend the barrel over your head and brain you. Jim," she spoke to her husband, "take care of the other one and make your sons proud of you."

The friend stepped back, and Donnelly and Farrell went at it; the first of their two destined fist fights.

There are various accounts of that first fight. Some say it was modified murder; that Farrell was literally beaten to pulp without striking a blow in his own defense. Others have it with Farrell giving a good account of himself, and for awhile looking as though he would be the winner. All agree it was a drawn-out, savage affair, but there is no doubt as to the final outcome, however. John Farrell was given a merciless beating as the Donnelly youngsters shrieked their delight; then he was hustled to the gateway where Jim Donnelly, perhaps recalling the "sore tail" threat, launched the powerful kick that sent his foe through the opening and sprawled him at the feet of his horse.

Johannah then challenged the friend but the latter made tracks. As the two men rode away, Farrell is said to have muttered through puffed lips, "The world isn't big enough for Donnelly and me. Some fine day one of us is bound to kill the other."

Having lost to Jim Donnelly in a battle of brawn, John Farrell sought help through legal procedure; he took his case to court.

In 1845, as elsewhere throughout the Province of Ontario and the entire Dominion, there were numerous squatters in the Lucan district who had never been molested. In many cases the original owners of the properties had failed to keep up the taxes, and in time the land reverted to the Crown. Again, long possession of the land was regarded by the courts as equivalent of a title. In Donnelly's case, while the law was mindful of the eight years he had worked the farm, it also realized the land was not legally his. The decision; Farrell was given fifty of the hundred acre farm, and Donnelly lost half the fruits of eight years labor. Naturally, the verdict of the court did not endear John Farrell to Jim Donnelly.

Several days after the decision, Jim and Johannah Donnelly, standing before their cabin and shading their eyes, saw the house of John Farrell being erected in one of the far front fields they had formerly called their own. Farrell, working like a Trojan to get his home and barn completed, told his helpers, "Every time I sink an axe into wood I keep wishin' it was that damn Donnelly's head."

The following two years were marked with constant quarrels between Farrell and Donnelly; there were many accusations but no further blows were struck. In the spring of 1856, Farrell found three of his cows poisoned and named Donnelly as the poisoner. Sufficient evidence was lacking to make a case of it. One night, in the fall of the same year, Farrell's barn mysteriously went up in flames; again suspicion pointed at the Donnellys, but once more there was not enough evidence to warrant an arrest.

Farrell voiced loud disapproval. "This is a hell of a land, were you can't have a man arrested just because you don't see him do what you know he did. Donnelly will be shooting at me next!"

Several months later, in mid-winter of 1857, someone did just that. One dusk as John Farrell sat down to his supper, a musket ball whizzed through one kitchen window and out another, missing his head by inches. Farrell seized his gun, threw open the kitchen door, fired into the darkness, loaded and fired again. He waited, listened, but heard nothing. Then he went to his stable, saddled a horse, galloped into Lucan and demanded the immediate arrest of his neighbor. The Lucan constable refused, saying he had no proof. "Who needs proof?" demanded Farrell. "It was Donnelly of course; him or one of those wild hellions of his. They're as black in sin as their father!"

His words coined the title, "The Black Donnellys."

In May 1857, several railroad men arrived in the Lucan area to begin surveying for a line. Excitement swept throughout the district; prosperity undreamed of seemed just around the corner. The following month Donnelly and Farrell met at that fatal logging bee.

It was the custom of Ontario farmers, as elsewhere in those days, to assist each other in erecting homes and barns. Meeting at an arranged site, each donated a day's labor. Invariably, considerable heavy drinking marked the occasion. Such was the case the day the two met at one of those communal efforts. Jim Donnelly, though he would take a drink as readily as the next man, usually knew when to stop. That day was the exception; he let down the bars. Finally, dropping his axe, the wobbly Donnelly had to sit down under a tree, head in hands in a drunken stupor.

The others continued on without him, drinking and working in relays. Of course the general conversation was the impending arrival of the railway, and its good to the community. Farrell, eyeing his enemy, noted the other's seemingly helpless condition. Farrell had downed his share but he wasn't drunk — "just enough in him to get ugly and remember past wounds." John Farrell suddenly held up a hand for silence. "The railroad will be a fine thing for the district," he spoke loudly, "but first we should rid it of some of its thieves and would-be murderers. One of them isn't far from me now; I can smell him from here."

Drunk he might have been, but Jim Donnelly heard the words and knew who they were meant for. He raised his head, then slowly got to his feet, eyes narrowed in one of those glares that made you "hear the sound of shovels digging your grave." He shouted, "If there's a thief around here, Farrell, you'll be the one to get the scent alright. Every skunk smells his own hole first!"

Farrell bounded forward, throwing down his axe; some later said he threw it at Donnelly but it missed its target. The next minute the two were at it again. This time, however, intoxication had robbed Jim Donnelly of his quick movements and the split-second timing of his punches. Farrell's first blow put him on his back, while the watching farmers cheered at the unusual sight and urged Farrell on. Cursing his foe and his own clumsiness, Jim Donnelly rose, walked into another punch and again felt the ground beneath him. But in falling, his hand came in contact with an iron bar. Springing to his feet and shouting, "Take this to hell with you!" he sent it crashing against the head of Farrell. The latter slumped to the ground, mortally wounded.

Still clutching the iron bar in a menacing manner and turning to the others, Donnelly, a bit pale, suddenly seemed quite sober. "The first one who lays a hand on me gets the same medicine," he warned to the semicircle of grim faces, and began a backward retreat to the roadway.

"Don't be a fool, Donnelly," spoke someone. "You're going with us to the constable. Throw down that bar or we'll take it away from you."

"The first one that tries, won't live to tell about it," was the answer. "Another murder won't make it any worse; they can only hang me once." Again the Donnelly glare was evident; it halted the others. He continued his backward retreat till he reached the roadway and his horse. Springing on it and shouting, "When you come for me, you'd better come shooting," Jim Donnelly slapped his horse on the rump, galloped up the roadway and was soon lost to sight.

CHAPTER THREE

They're Going to Hang Jim Donnelly

Two years in woods behind his farm,
Donnelly hid from his foes,
And worked his fields with his sons,
Dressed in a woman's clothes.
— Old Song

The Roman Line, the once so notorious road that leads past the old Donnelly place — and so named because of the many Irish Roman Catholic families that settled along its borders — was the scene of numerous grim escapades and arsons in the days when Lucan was known as "the wildest spot in Canada." A story, popular during the Donnelly feud, tells of a stranger, traveling by horse and buggy and looking for the Donnelly farmhouse, who stopped a local inhabitant to inquire if he was on the right road.

"This is it, the Roman Line," was the unhesitant answer. "The farther down the road you go, the tougher the folks get, and the Donnellys live in the last house."

In later life Johannah Donnelly, telling of her husband's return to the farm following his fatal battle with John Farrell, informed, "I had young Tom across my knees, warming his behind when Jim rode up. As a little one,

23

Tom was a bit of a cry-baby when his older brothers were teaching him to fight; but he's grown up to be a foin young man who'd slap the devil in the face. A credit to all of us."

During his twenty-five years of life, the "credit to all of us," Tom Donnelly, was arrested five times on charges of brawling, robbery and arson, and had been accused of attempted murder. At the time he was murdered and his head chopped off, he was under bonds to appear at the Spring Assizes on a charge of robbing a post office. Not that there was anything unusual about a criminal charge in the Donnelly household. In the Spring Assizes of 1876, there were thirteen true bills against the Donnellys; charges of incendiarism, poisoning and highway robbery. On the very morning Johannah and Jim Donnelly were murdered, they were scheduled to appear in the court at Granton on an arson charge.

When Jim Donnelly reached home after his final brawl with Farrell, he flung open the door and announced to his wife, "I've just killed John Farrell! I've got to get out of here, have to travel far and fast!"

Johannah's jaw dropped. Murder was different than a common brawl; trouble could come from it.

Donnelly saw the pathetic gazes of his eight children. At that time James Jr., the oldest, was not quite fifteen. Briefly, Donnelly told what had happened, then stepped to the front door and looked up the road towards Stephen Township, the scene of his recent battle. When trouble came, he knew it would come from that direction. He turned to his wife.

"They may be on their way here now. Farrell was well liked, and you know how every damn one of them feel about me."

"If they get you, Jim, they'll take you to jail."

"If they get me they won't bother to take me to jail — just up to the nearest tree." Then he asked, "How much money is there in the house?"

The eyes of Johannah Donnelly had been narrowed in thought.

"Wait, Jim," she spoke. "We have only a bit of silver and you know it. You can't hope to get far with that, and if you run away you'll be doin' the very thing they expect you to do. Let's use our heads."

He eyed her in surprise. "What would you have me do?"

She pointed towards the heavily wooded area that began a short distance from the house. (Little or none is left of the woods today.)

"There's your answer, Jim," she went on. "Hide out there in the woods. When they come to get you. I'll tell them you've gone far away and I don't know where you are. They'll never search for you in the woods, and we can feed you."

Donnelly wanted to know how.

"Every night I'll put two candles in the window, along about midnight," informed Johannah. "That will mean it's safe to come here. If you see three candles, you'll know that someone is here or else I smell danger, and you are to stay away that night. There may be several nights, there may be many of them that you'll have to stay away; you'll probably miss many a meal but it's better than having your neck stretched."

She gave further instructions while hurriedly preparing a basket of provisions. Jim Donnelly secured his musket and loaded himself with ammunition. Several of the boys went to the roadway to report of any approach. It was seven-year old Mike Donnelly who found his father's hunting knife and gave it to him. Something prophetic there.

Mike was later to go down, fighting to the last, with a hunting knife buried deep in his back.

Ready to leave, Donnelly kissed his wife, his little daughter Jennie and the boys goodbye. Picking up club-footed William, who was twelve at the time, he said, "Your father has to leave you for awhile, but don't believe what they will tell you about him. If you had been in my boots, you would have done the same thing."

There is little reason to doubt those words. Despite the many terrible accusations that were to be hurled against the Donnellys in future years, it was William who was always referred to as "the worst of the whole damn lot," as well as "that fiddling devil of a cripple." It seems that William, when not watching the crops, homes and barns of his enemies go up in flames, was a backwoods violinist of sorts.

While John Farrell did not die immediately at the hands of Jim Donnelly, he never regained consciousness and expired three days later.

Not until then was a warrant issued for Donnelly's arrest. The reason for such delay is not certain; but the fact remains that John Farrell was being placed in his coffin, worm-fodder for the future, before the Lucan constable, accompanied by several angry farmers, rode up to the Donnelly farmhouse. They were met at the door by the grim and scowling Johannah, who asked, "What do you want?"

The constable said they wanted her husband.

"He isn't here," was her reply. "As for John Farrell, Jim had to do it; it was a case of kill or be killed. And you'll never find Jim. He's gone far away, and I wouldn't tell you where even if I did know. Now get to hell off this farm."

The constable then questioned the young Donnelly boys, but they remained sphinx-like in silence. Johannah had coached her brood well.

There were a few half-hearted attempts made to find him, but on the whole no murderer was ever less bothered by pursuit than Jim Donnelly. The following five months found him hidden in the woods, and less than a hundred rods from his home. In the daytime, high in the branches of a tree or peering from the thick brush, he could see the smoke rising from the chimney and his children playing in the yard; could hear the crowing of roosters, the whinnying of the horses, the lowing of his cows, and had the occasional glimpses of Johannah on one of her endless trips to the barn, pump or woodshed, as the farmlife went on without him.

Every midnight saw two burning candles on the table near the kitchen window; it meant all was well, he had warm meals, a few minutes with Johannah and left with the food that lasted him through the daytime.

Then winter set in and Donnelly moved from the woods to burrow into the hayloft in his barn. It was lonely, cold and monotonous, with each hour seemingly a day, but it was safe. Another two months went by and still no evidence of danger. He began to think there would be no further efforts made to catch him. But one night in February 1858, with snow deep on the surrounding fields and winter winds whistling, Jim Donnelly had stolen from the barn and was making tracks towards his house, when he saw that which brought him to a sharp halt. Three candles were burning in the window!

Johannah had unwelcome visitors that night.

Somehow, despite the comparative isolation of the farmhouse and the lateness of the hours, Donnelly had eventually been seen by some passerby as he approached the house. In fact the Lucan constable had several reports of the lone figure that made its way to the farmhouse at the midnight hour. He decided an investigation was in order. So one night, accompanied by two deputies and all of them armed, the constable made an unexpected call at the Donnelly home.

Leaving their horses at a neighboring farmer's, the three men covered the last half-mile in darkness and silence and walked in on the surprised Johannah around 10 p.m.

The constable wasted no time on preliminaries. Word had reached him of the one who came to the house after midnight; he wanted to know the identity of the caller, all information on same and what she had to say about the matter. Johannah said plenty, beginning her address with the endearing phrase, "Listen, you three snooping bastards!" Her speech, summed up briefly, told the constable he was all wet in his suspicions of her having any midnight visitors, and that, "I have no male callers; I wouldn't let any man climb into bed with me."

The constable, watching her mannish, scowling features, might have wondered what man in his right mind would have wanted to climb into bed with her, but that's just an opinion.

He did, however, make it evident that he didn't believe her. Johannah, her brood put to bed, was alone in the kitchen at the time the three entered. But the limb of the law took no chances. He sent one of his deputies to keep watch on the sleeping boys; he placed another in a strategic position that hid the man from any outside view through the windows. Then sitting down beside the kitchen door, a long dueling pistol across his knees, while Johannah glared daggers, he informed her that John Farrell had been a very good friend of his, and that he and the deputies intended to "stick around for awhile and see what happens."

Johannah said nothing; she made herself comfortable in a chair by the stove — and waited.

A long silence followed, one that seemed to stand out as though held there in a frame. On a homemade shelf, a clock ticked out the minutes as time passed. Snowflakes swirled up to and flattened themselves on the windows; wind gusts whipped over and against the house. The Lucan constable, seemingly content, smoked his pipe and waited. It was well after eleven when the silence was broken. From the neighboring farmyard of Pat "Grouchy" Ryder came the distant, drawn-out bay of a hound that was repeated several times. The gaze of the constable went to Johannah. "It's a bad night to be out and maybe a dangerous one," he opined. "Some people say that the bay of a hound foretells death."

There was no answer and silence was resumed, except for the endless "tick-tick-tick-tick" of the clock.

With midnight less than thirty minutes away, Johannah Donnelly rose, threw wood into the stove and placed a filled tea-kettle on it — the eyes of the others watching her in dull interest. With the kettle singing she brought butter, a loaf of bread and a shoulder of ham from the cupboard. The three men beamed; their recent ride and more recent walk through the cold night made food a welcome sight. Muttering something about needing more light, Johannah lit a half-dozen candles, then the constable, with chow seemingly in the offing, became gallant and asked if he could be of assistance. At her request he obligingly put three candles on the table in front of the window.

Johannah must have got a whale of a kick out of that, and it was one for the books — John Law himself warning the fugitive and telling him to stay away. Who says there is nothing new under the sun?

Her purpose accomplished and without arousing comment, Johannah cut off and fried a generous slice of ham along with butter-covered eggs made two Dagwood-size sandwiches, a pot of tea, then sat down and polished it all off — while the three uninvited looked on. The hint of one hungry deputy, "That ham smells good," only brought the reply, "It tastes even better." The trio remained till well after 2 a.m., but neither Jim Donnelly nor anyone else made an appearance. Later that winter — 1858 — and on two other occasions, the Lucan constable made unexpected visits to the Donnelly farmhouse, but in each case he was obliged to leave without the wanted man — and hungry.

Somehow, when others were present, Johannah always managed to get the three warning candles in the window without arousing suspicion.

Spring came and Jim Donnelly returned to the woods at the back of his farm, where he continued to remain till seeding time. Then complications arose in the form of man shortage.

Time for the plow and harrow, Johannah came down with a severe case of grippe. With the boys still too young and inexperienced to be of much help in the fields, and the usually obliging neighbors shunning the place — few if any of them wished to mingle with the family of a murderer — Jim Donnelly was faced with the problem of spring planting. He solved it by impersonating his wife. Johannah was almost as tall and heavy as her husband; apparelled in her clothes, Donnelly was taken for her by those traveling the road and seeing him in the fields, and was able to get in the seeding. Later, still dressed in a woman's clothing, he brought in the crops, working with his sons, and did the fall plowing.

Snow again and once more Donnelly burrowed in the hay in his barn, exiled from humanity. The longer winter months dragged along, then came spring of 1859 and Jim Donnelly had enough of hiding. He walked into Lucan and surrendered.

As John Farrell had been murdered in Huron County's Stephen Township, Jim Donnelly was tried at the Huron Assizes. The trial attracted considerable attention, for although Donnelly himself was not too well known in the Huron district at that time, his name was, as well as the manner in which he had evaded capture. People wanted to see the man who had outwitted the law for more than a year and "worked his fields, with his sons, dressed in a woman's clothes." He pleaded self-defense, but there had been more than a score of witnesses to the murder. He was sentenced to be hanged. That night Lucan buzzed with the news. "They're going to hang Jim Donnelly."

But they never did. The verdict was changed to seven years imprisonment.

Before he was taken away to serve his sentence, he was allowed to speak with his wife. "I'll be back. Never forget that and never let my boys forget it. I'll be back. And when I do — ." He broke off in the middle of the sentence, the eyes of Jim and Johannah Donnelly met. A few minutes later he was on his way to prison.

CHAPTER FOUR

The Fires Begin to Break Out

By thefts they showed their father's blood
By fights and drunken sprees;
Till the countryside, lying in dread,
Called them The Black Donnellys.
— Old Song

Today a schoolhouse stands near the old Donnelly place.
It was built on the site of the one attended by the seven
sons of Jim Donnelly. The original structure, like other
frontier temples of learning, must have been the scene of
some God-awful classroom boners and mutilations of the
King's English. Many who learned their A-B-C's there
were to become bitter foes of the Donnellys. A party of
raiders once met behind it before attacking the Donnelly
farmhouse; and for some years those hallowed halls were
graced or disgraced — take your pick — with the presence
of one Willie Dunnegan.

True stories even remotely connected with the Donnellys of Lucan that have the faintest semblance of humor,
are as rare as tickets to heaven. The story of Willie Dunnegan is the exception.

Besides being the class dunce, it seems that the presence of Willie could have been detected by a blind man, if

the latter's olfactory organ did but a fifth of its duty. In Willie's case, the perfumes of Araby were conspicuous by their absence. Briefly, Willie stunk. In fact, one warm day with nary a breeze blowing, his personal aroma became so predominant that the teacher sent him home to his mother with the note that read:

"Dear Mrs. Dunnegan: Please wash Willie. He smells."

The mother had the Celtic temperament and sharp wit of her ancestors. She scribbled a few words and sent Willie back to the long-suffering pedagog with the answering note: "Dear Teacher: Teach Willie and don't smell him. He's no rose!"

During his seven years imprisonment, the wife and sons of Jim Donnelly carried on the work of the farm and actually improved the family's financial status.

Johannah, herself ambitious and able to do a man's work, was a tireless taskmaker and the boys obeyed her without question. No number of hours in the fields were too many, no task impossible if she but asked it. In later years such obedience was the cause of most of the trouble, for as time marched on few of Johannah's orders had anything to do with the welfare of the farm or family. They were mostly concerned with the destruction of the farm and family life of others. Old Johannah hated peace, but to the sons it was a case of "Mother knows best," and her commands were the law.

There is, however, one good deed recorded of her. Something or other a neighboring woman did, pleased her, and as a reward Johannah informed the other, "I like you, so you won't have to worry as long as I continue to like you. I'll not tell my sons to burn you out."

There now — wasn't that nice of her?

True, with their father in jail, the boys were frequently the butt of cruel remarks with regard to the cause of his absence, but as they grew older they were able to avenge all insults with their fists — and how! The Donnellys were not gunfighters, had a strange aversion to firearms and seldom touched them; but without exception the entire seven of them, as well as the father, were veritable terrors, wild men in fist and club battles, who when fighting, according to Detective Hugh McKinnon, former Chief of Police at Belleville, "became as howling maniacs, resembling nothing human, while snarling, clawing and biting with the fury of wild beasts at bay."

On one occasion three of the Donnellys put eleven thieving gypsies to flight. On another, eight of them made John Flannigan and seventeen of his supporters take to their heels. They feared no man and it was only when hopelessly outnumbered that they ever lost a "rough-and-tumble" — with one exception. That exception was the one man who could handle any of them, feared none of them and was destined to bring destruction to most of them. But more of that man later.

For two years after Jim Donnelly's imprisonment, all was calm in the Lucan area. But the feeling of the inhabitants of the surrounding countryside did not mellow with the passing of time. To them Jim Donnelly was still a thief and a murderer, and it was always predicted of his seven sons that, "when they get older their bad blood will show." As it turned out, buckets of blood were to show before the feud was over.

Jim Donnelly had served almost three years of his sentence when the barn of a farmer, living a good ten miles from the Donnelly homestead, mysteriously went up in flames one night. The farmer was a very puzzled as well as irate man. Everything about the fire pointed to a case of arson, but to the best of his knowledge he had no enemies; certainly no one could have hated him to such an extent as to cause him to lose his barn and three of his best horses. At least, that's what he thought.

The very next night the unknown arsonists struck again; once more flames leaped skyward while the house of the neighbor, whose fields bordered the acres of the first victim, was burned to the ground, and its inmates barely escaped with their lives. Two weeks later the barn of a third farmer named McMahon was burned during the night, the fire spreading to a nearby shed and resulting in the loss of a considerable amount of farming equipment and livestock.

Surprise, then fear swept over the countryside.

There were several meetings and theories were advanced. While at first it might have been thought that fire number one could have been caused by neglect or some freak accident, the speedy repetition of the second and third could mean only one thing, it was decided. Vandals were in the vicinity. Numerous farmers, armed and ready, took to keeping an all night watch behind the unlit windows of their houses. Others waited through the hours of darkness in their barns, ready to greet any prowler with hot lead.

But the days passed into weeks, the weeks into months — and no more fires. At length, the danger apparently over, vigilance laxed. But speculation continued as to the reason for the three fires. It was several months after their occurence when someone recalled an interesting coincidence and voiced it. Oddly enough, the three men who had suffered at the hands of the arsonists were all present at the murder of John Farrell, that day at the logging bee, and had been the principal witnesses against Jim Donnelly at the latter's trial. The man who recalled and voiced the fact was one Robert McLean, whose hatred for "that bad Donnelly bunch" was well known.

His comments threw a new light on the mystery of the fires; a few days later the Lucan constable again made tracks for the Donnelly house. Questions were in order. Three years had passed since his last visit to the farm.

The first thing that must have struck the officer was the tangible fact that the sons of Jim Donnelly were growing up — and fast. James Jr., the eldest, now twenty and already a husky six-footer, was sitting on the front steps. Seventeen-year-old William, "sprouting up like a weed and practicing on his fiddle" — and perhaps keeping time with his club-foot — was in the house with fifteen-year-old John and the others, Patrick, Michael, Robert and Thomas. Tom, the youngest of the boys, was eventually to be the acclaimed 'muscle-man' of the family. There was no friendly greetings for the constable; the sons of Jim Donnelly regarded him with narrowed eyes and in frowning silence.

Johannah loudly denied that her brood had anything to do with the fires. "You're just trying to make trouble for me and my little angels, now that my good man is not here to protect us," was her assertion.

As it turned out, Johannah didn't need her husband to protect her, one of the "little angels" was well able to supply all the protection needed. The constable only had time for a few questions when he felt the strong arm that seized his shoulder, wheeled him around, and he was gazing into the hard eyes of James Jr., who said, "You've done enough talking. Mother told you we had nothing to do with those fires, and that means we had nothing to do with them. But we do know who started all the rumors; it was that damn Bob McLean."

"McLean only said it was strange that the barns fired were those of the three principal witnesses against your father at his trial," put in the other. "Every man has a right to his opinion."

James Donnelly, grim, nodded. "Good. That gives me a right to mine, which is that McLean is looking for trouble and you're begging for it. A few years ago you were out here several times looking for my father and making a damn nuisance of yourself. That's when us boys were just a bunch of frightened kids and couldn't do anything. Well, some of us aren't kids any longer, soon none of us will be, so I'm telling you to get to hell off this place and stay off. And just in case you forget — remember this!"

James Donnelly's right fist lashed out with the sudden and unexpected blow that caught the surprised constable flush on the jaw and downed him. The others surged forward, but the older brother shouted for them to stay back, saying that he didn't need any help, then proceeded to "put the boots" to the one at his feet. It wasn't to be the only time that a law officer received similar treatment at Donnelly hands — and feet. At least six other Lucan constables were given beatings, some of them fearful ones, by the Donnellys. One of their victims eventually lost his sight. In fact, in time the position of Lucan constable became about as safe as a pork chop with a hungry lion, and as desirable as skunk at a picnic.

Bleeding and groggy after a vicious going over, and with his badge pinned to the seat of his pants, the Lucan constable was hustled through the Donnelly gateway in a manner similar to that of John Farrell five years earlier. Amid jeers, the officer got on his horse, while Johannah, proud and defiant, watched from the doorway, and the fists of her wild brood were raised as they dared the constable to ever return. Two nights later the barn of Robert McLean was burned to the ground. The following week four of his cattle were poisoned and three of his horses were found with their throats cut.

Yes, the Donnelly boys were growing up!

In the spring of the next year — 1863 — numerous petty thefts began to occur in the Lucan area. Farmers complained of harness and farm implements disappearing from sheds and barns; village storekeepers told of locked doors being forced open, of looted money boxes and stolen merchandise. There were several cases of village topers, when well-oiled and making an unsteady way homeward, being strong-armed by masked young hoodlums, beaten unconscious and robbed.

All the thefts and attacks, rightly or wrongly, were popularly attributed to the sons of Jim Donnelly, although no formal charges were brought against them.

It was sometime during the summer of that year when the "strangled dog" incident occured. It was inevitable that being handsome as well as fearless, the Donnelly boys were greatly admired by girls of their own age. Somehow this went double in spades for William, despite his club-foot. Thus in the summer of 1863, William, then seventeen, was found leaning over a gate, making talk with a farmer's daughter.

It is one thing to steal a man's possessions, poison his cattle or burn down his barn, but it is another to tamper with his daughter's affections. The father, arriving unexpectedly upon the scene and seeing his daughter gaily chatting with a hated Donnelly, came bolting to the rescue as though she were being menaced by a snake.

William was not aware of the other's presence till a big fist sent him crashing to the ground, where the farmer fully expected him to remain. It showed that he did not know William Donnelly, or any of the Donnellys for that matter, very well. When once in a fight a Donnelly never quit till either he was dead, or his foe bleeding and unconscious. Still lying on his back, William Donnelly launched the kick that lifted the farmer into the air. The next instant he was on his feet and "putting the boots" to the fallen man.

The horrified girl screamed; she saw the same look in William's eyes that Farrell had seen in Jim Donnelly's eyes before he died.

The girl's screams brought the farm collie, a huge vicious brute, racing to the scene. The dog's first rush knocked William off his feet, and then the dog whirled in for his throat. The suddenly freed farmer got up, saw his chance and booted William's head. Without saying a word — a Donnelly never asked, gave nor expected mercy — young William fought his way to his feet. He had a sort of shuffling dance he used when he fought; and after the manner of French-Canadian lumberjacks, his feet were as fast and more dangerous than his fists. The farmer and his dog fell back, inside their gate, with William outside, his chest heaving, his eyes icy cold. Then he turned on his heel and walked away.

The farmer thought he had won.

None of the Donnellys were ones to let anyone hold the illusion he had won over them. William Donnelly returned to the farmhouse late that night, a rope in his pocket, a knife in his belt. Not wishing to get shot, Donnelly kept in the shadows where his rustling noises soon attracted the attention of the dog. The brute caught his scent, recognized it as that of an enemy and rushed him with a throaty snarl. William met the charge head-on, ready this time. His hands locked in the matted fur throat, his grip tightened. Teeth snapped within inches of his face, but he held on. Not until the animal was dead did William Donnelly release his hold. Then — so the story goes — he whipped out his knife and cut out the dog's eyes.

This done, he put a noose around the dog's neck and hung him to a limb of a tree in the farmer's front yard, where it was certain to be seen — a grim symbol of Donnelly vengeance!

Lucan's first fire of any consequence destroyed Conroy's Mechanic's Hall on November 16, 1862. It's second fire, the destruction of Madill's Hotel, in February 1865, is said to have been brought around, indirectly, by the curiosity of a cattle drover, who happened to stop over at the hotel for the night.

For some months before the fire the hotel proprietor, Mike Madill, had been buying meat for his place from James Donnelly Jr. There came the evening when young Donnelly entered the hotel lobby and passed through it, on his way to the kitchen, a quarter of beef across one shoulder. A cattle drover, well-known in the district and seated in the lobby watched him as he passed then turned to Madill.

"That's one of those Black Donnellys, isn't it? Don't tell me you buy your meat from him, one of a family of unhung thieves and the son of a murderer."

Madill shrugged, demanded to know what was wrong about that and pointed out, "Just because the family has a bad name doesn't mean the meat is bad. Young Donnelly came in here awhile back, offered to supply me with meat at lower prices than I was paying, so I started buying from him. So far we've got along alright and I have no complaints." Then he informed, "I understand he also supplies the hotel at Granton."

"He must have a good size herd?"

"I don't know anything about that. I'm satisfied and that's all that concerns me."

The drover smoked on in silence, but he must have been doing a lot of thinking. The following night, returning from a day's visit to surrounding farms, he drew Madill to one side. "Mike, I took it on myself to do a little checking up today, while I was out inspecting herds," he told the other. "I talked to several farmers living near the Donnelly place and got the same answer from all of them. James Donnelly Jr. has been supplying both your hotel and the Granton House with meat since early fall, at least five months ago."

"What of it?"

"Just this. During the last five months not a Donnelly cow has calved. The herd is exactly the same size it was in the fall, neither larger or smaller by one head; yet young Donnelly has been supplying two hotels with meat for five months and he still has the same amount of cattle he had in the fall. Something wrong there, don't you think?"

The other regarded him. "So?"

"So add to that the fact that several farmers in this district have recently had a cow stolen from them, and you can see what I'm driving at."

Madill's eyes widened as a thought struck him. "You — you think that the meat he has been selling me is —"

The drover nodded. "That's just what I do think."

Madill was a fiery upholder of the law, with little patience for its transgressors. When James Donnelly made his next call at the hotel, he was loudly told to "get to hell out of here with your stolen meat, you black thief!" Donnelly denied the meat was stolen; he said it was from his own herd but he couldn't explain why the size of that same herd never decreased. Finally, putting down the beef he carried, he told Madill he was going to wipe up the floor with him and send him to his grave a cripple. But the rising voices of the two brought several farmers from the nearby bar; when the cause of the argument was made known, rage swept over the listeners. They came forward and grabbed the accused. James Donnelly was not only thrown out of the hotel and kicked numerous times, "given a dose of his own medicine," the cry was raised that he should be publicly horsewhipped, then and there.

Somehow he managed to get to his horse and ride out of the village with his skin still intact.

Four nights later, around 3 a.m. on February 17, 1865, Madill's Hotel became a sea of flames that burned to the ground. Undoubtedly it was the work of arsonists though their identity was never proven; but rumor had it that some awakened housewives on the Roman Line heard the sound of galloping hooves, hurrying towards the Donnelly place in the wee cold hours before the dawn!

CHAPTER FIVE

The Return of Jim Donnelly

Jim Donnelly served his years in jail,
Then he returned one fall,
To find his seven handsome sons,
Grown big and strong and tall.

— Old Song

The Lucan flag-pole was erected May 9, 1863. In April 1865 the flag was placed at half-mast in respect to Abraham Lincoln, and there was mourning for the man who had been admired by the entire community. Johannah Donnelly is quoted as having said, "There must have been some Irish in him, somewhere." In 1873 the flagpole was cut down by unknown vandals. Of course to the Lucan area it had to be, "the work of the Black Donnellys." To most of the populace of the district, no matter what happened or where it happened — Mary could have had another little lamb — it was "the work of the Black Donnellys."

In the spring of 1866 a field day was held at London, seventeen miles from Lucan, where cash prizes were offered to the winners of the running, jumping, shot-put, caber-tossing and other contests of brawn and endurance.

With money in the offing, the Donnelly boys journeyed to the London games. Nineteen-year-old John Donnelly won the one-mile race, and later in the day the two-
mile run, with brother Pat a close second in both events.
James Jr., though he had never beheld a caber before in
his life, tossed the big pole farther than the ten or so
muscular and experienced Scots competing against him,
claimed the prize money then remarked that the sport
could only have been thought up by "some damn fool
Scotchman." One of his defeated competitors heard the
words, resented them and fists flew, the battle ending with
the son of the land of the heather flat on his back and
helpless. According to Detective Hugh McKinnon, the sons
of Jim Donnelly "won nineteen of the twenty-one contests
held that day, then hurried back to their hard-eyed mother,
pockets jingling with silver dollars."

It was the same Detective McKinnon who, after the
Donnelly massacre, was quoted by a reporter of the Globe
as saying, "Hundreds of people are cheering at the news
of the massacre and you can't blame them. The Donnellys
were not humans, only mad dogs that look like humans —
wild things that should have lived before the cave men.
Everyone is bettered, now that the Donnellys are wiped
out!"

On a fall day in 1866, the late afternoon stage from
London rumbled into Lucan and pulled up before Fitzhenry's Hotel. The arrival of the stage always caused a
certain excitement. It brought the papers from London,
news from the outside and the occasional newcomer. That
was to be a red-letter day, as excitement goes. One of the
passengers that stepped from the stage was certainly no
newcomer to Lucan, though his appearance caused a series
of exclamations among the idlers before the hotel. Pres-

ently, several of them were hurrying along the street to inform the village of the identity of the stage's recent passenger.

After seven year's absence and having completed his sentence, Jim Donnelly was returning to Lucan, grim and sinister as ever. The passing years had added a few whisps of gray to his once coal black hair and prison pallor was noticeable; but there was still that something which warned he was not the man to take liberties with, and the Donnelly glare was evident.

He entered Fitzhenry's bar, ordered a drink and was served while its occupants drew back, eyeing him in silence. So Jim Donnelly had finally come back, eh?

There were no friendly greetings, no "welcome home" or "have one on me", offers from any of those who had known him so long. But the same thought was in the minds of all. Now that he had returned, what did he intend to do? What would come next? After a long silence and as Donnelly filled his glass for the third time, the bartender, Dan McKenna, put in, "None of us have been seeing you around here for quite awhile, Donnelly."

Jim Donnelly's eyes went to those of McKenna. "I intend to take care of that, all in good time," was the answer. He downed his drink, put the glass back on the bar and added, "There won't be any complaints about my absence. Everyone around here will be seeing lots of me, maybe more than any of you want to see of me, when the right time comes. You can be damn sure of that."

"What do you intend to do?" McKenna wanted to know.

"What do you think I should do?"

"I haven't any idea," answered Dan McKenna.

Jim Donnelly made no reply. He tossed a coin onto the bar and walked out into the street, just in time to see the plunging horses and the heavy farm wagon that careened around the corner and carried his seven husky sons, hurrying to meet him. A series of howls arose that would have done credit to an attacking Indian war-party, as their eyes fell upon him. The next minute they were all milling around their father with rough hugs, back-slapping and handshakes; while Jim Donnelly, gaping in surprise, seemed unable to believe the change seven years had made. These were no longer little boys; they were tall, rowdy and reckless young men, aware of the fear they inspired in others.

That fear was evident within seconds after their arrival in the village. As the sons of Jim Donnelly made their appearance and a wave of shouts arose, shopping housewives who had met and were gossiping on the streets, suddenly took wings of flight homeward, while sunbonnets rocked and bustles rustled. Village loiterers either remembered urgent business elsewhere, or stepped within the door of the building nearest to them. In fact, in less than sleight-of-hand time the streets were deserted, except for the fourteen-year old boy from nearby Huron County, who sat in a buggy before a feed store. In later life he told a reporter:

"That was the first time I laid eyes on the Donnellys and I won't forget it. Nobody that was there would. Dad had driven over to Lucan, taken me with him and had gone into the feed store, when I saw a man step out of Fitzhenry's Hotel. Then a wagon came around the corner, with seven young fellows in it. At the sight of the man they cheered so loud I had to pull reins on our horse. They sprang from the wagon and ran towards the man. They acted like wild Indians and they all seemed half-crazy.

"One of them — I am not sure which one but I believe it was Mike — picked up a chair before the window of

Molony's Wagon-Shop, sent it crashing through the window and shouted to the others, 'That's just to let some the village bastards know we've been here'!" Later as Dad drove me home, he told me the man was Jim Donnelly, who had murdered John Farrell years before, and had just got out of jail. I had only been a toddler then, but I remembered hearing of it. Dad said the young fellows were the sons of Jim Donnelly, a bad lot, and that the country could do well without such a family. Of course I had heard of the Black Donnellys."

The name of the boy who sat in the buggy that day, and saw the sons of Jim Donnelly arrive to meet their father, was James Carroll. Keep that name — James Carroll — in mind. You will be reading more of the one destined to be known as "the only man who didn't fear the Black Donnellys."

Among others who had witnessed the murder of John Farrell and testified against Jim Donnelly at the latter's trial, was a farmer named Haskett. Around midnight, on the very day Jim Donnelly returned to his family, several masked riders rode up to Haskett's barn, "whooping like savages," and threw burning faggots into the hayloft before riding away, while the terrorized Haskett remained within the house — "My life wouldn't have been worth a copper if I went outside."

While Haskett was able to save his horses, the barn burned to embers.

CHAPTER SIX

John Law Steps In

You could put a Black Donnelly in jail,
But you couldn't keep one there.
Men feared to speak against them,
Much to the law's despair.

— Old Song

It was shortly after the Donnelly feud was brought to it's sudden and drastic climax, that a newspaper man asked a prominent resident of Biddulph Township, "Who was the worst of the Donnellys?" The other, evidently a Shakespeare spouter, mulled the question for a moment then quoted the bard in answering:

"There's small choice in rotten apples."

Detective Hugh McKinnon had his own views of the question. "The old woman was the instigator of most of the trouble, the master-mind of the outfit and gave all the orders. Of the boys, William was the most eager to carry them out, with Tom and Mike a tie for second place. Forgetting daughter Jennie, an unusually beautiful and quiet girl, Patrick was the only one of the Donnellys, including the mother and father, that never stood before a judge. Five of the Donnellys served prison sentences.."

McKinnon should have known; as a guest with his true identity a secret, he once spent a week at the Donnelly farmhouse.

For several years after Jim Donnelly returned to his family, he and his sons continued to terrorize the Biddulph district. There were numerous street brawls and sideroad gang fights, all of which were won by the Donnellys. There were several other cases of poisoned cattle and arson; all of them were rumored as being the handiwork of the bad boys of Biddulph. By this time, so appalling was the dread of them, that no one in the area would dare press charges against the Donnellys for fear of reprisals. There were a number of cases of families, fed up with fear, that moved out of the district.

There was the case of farmer Joseph Ryan, long a victim of Donnelly perpetrations, who was finally beaten to a pulp one night by Tom Donnelly and robbed of eighty dollars. Desperate, when Ryan finally went to the authorities at Lucan to seek help, he was told, "If the Donnellys are against you, all Biddulph can't help you!"

No one suffered more at Donnelly hands than one Joseph Casswell. There came the summer when Casswell was unable to get thrashers to help him with his harvest. Knowing of the Donnelly hatred for Casswell, none would assist him in the fields fearing dire consequences at Donnelly hands. Faced with ruin if he could not get in his harvest, Casswell finally went to the parish priest, asking if he would intercede for him with the Donnellys. The good man agreed and driving over to the place, asked Jim Donnelly to allow the thrashers to come in and help Casswell. After a few minutes silence, Donnelly's answer was that he would think the matter over and mail his reply.

A few days later the priest received the letter that contained the one word: "No!"

Canada's first Dominion Parliament assembled at Ottawa on November 6, 1867, to begin making laws for a young Government. In the same month and year, James Donnelly Jr. followed the example of his sire twenty years earlier. He "squatted" on privately owned land, built a small log house and the following spring began breaking ground for his own farm.

Nothing shy or hesitant about a Donnelly.

For the following two years, word occasionally reached the outside world of the lawlessness and terror that prevailed in the Biddulph district. Among other stories were those of the four succeeding Lucan constables, who had been given merciless beatings by the Donnellys, and told to "make tracks, damn you — and don't come back!" Three of them did just that, after promptly resigning their jobs. One hadn't bothered to resign.

Eventually it became evident that outside help was needed. From Caledonia, in June 1870, Detective Hugh McKinnon of Criminal Investigation was sent to Lucan to bring around order and arrest its violators.

A better man could not have been selected for the job. McKinnon was an experienced and tireless sleuth, who had been the nemesis of many a criminal. He had brains as well as brawn. From the stories that had reached him, McKinnon knew that the principal reason for such lawlessness around Lucan was the fear inspired by the bad boys of Biddulph; its inhabitants were afraid to press charges against them. Plainly, it was necessary to prove the guilt of the terrorists; to get them dead-to-right. How, then, could this be better done — with his identity unknown — than to mingle with said terrorists, to know their every move and, perhaps, even get invited to their home?

Good. He would strike up an acquaintance with the Donnellys — somehow!

Then a stroke of luck played into his hands. Arriving in London, McKinnon learned that another field day was to be held there shortly. This was his chance! The information he had on the sons of Jim Donnelly was enough to inform that they were certain to be there; they were not the ones to pass up what was, for them, a way to make easy money. By competing against them he would meet them; by offering stiff competition he might gain their respect.

Now all this conjuncture was quite possible. McKinnon, a strapping six-footer and tipping the beam around the hundred and ninety mark, was an athlete of note with trophies to prove it. One of his shot-put efforts held a record for some years.

So on the field, that long-gone day, McKinnon first saw and met the seven bad boys of Biddulph — the wild sons of Jim Donnelly, as well as their sire, who had journeyed to London, accompanied by Johannah, to cheer them on — and to take their cash winnings. "There were twenty-three events that day," the detective later recalled. "I won three of them; two more were taken by London men. The other eighteen — . They were all won by the Donnelly boys."

Posing as a man of means from Ottawa, "out for some fun and excitement," he struck up an acquaintance with the Donnellys, after proving his brawn on the athletic field. The fact that the sleuth's mother had the foresight to be born near the Galty Mountains, in Southern Tipperary — Johannah's own birthplace — put him in the good graces of the old gal. Johannah, it seems, knew his mother back on the auld sod. McKinnon made the most out of that, and if he did tell a few little white lies to her, it was all in the performance of duty.

The following week found him travelling around Lucan, where he again met the Donnellys and at last hit pay-dirt. He was invited out to the farm "for a few days." He stretched it into a week and learned plenty.

At that time, along with clubfooted William, James Jr. was living on his own farm — at least they were the acres he had settled on and called his own — but a few miles from the old homestead. The brothers Patrick, Robert, Mike, John and Tom, stayed at the house of Jim and Johannah, along with pretty and seldom seen daughter Jennie. The rare appearances of Jennie in Lucan, brought secret sighs from rural Romeos, and undoubtedly she would have had many suitors at the house were it not for her family. Few if any sons of the sod were brave enough to enter the lion's den, even for such a juicy morsel as Jennie.

Oddly enough, the exception to the rule was William Farrell, the son of the man who had been murdered by Jim Donnelly. Seemingly the Donnelly boys tolerated him, perhaps in view of past circumstances, but William Farrell was never able to get as far as first base with their lovely sister. When love finally did come to her, it was in the apearance of a young man from the town of St. Thomas, some thirty miles to the south, who was able to meet the rigid requirements of Johannah and the family.

"That week at the Donnelly farmhouse was a nightmare." McKinnon later told. "It was like being in the combination of a boiler factory and a madhouse. If there was one full moment of quiet during my stay there, I cannot recall it."

It seems that when the boys were not fighting or slugging others, they were constantly practicing among themselves with no punches pulled. The house rang almost continuously with their shouts. Arguments and bickerings were frequent; fists flew and blows landed for little reason and sometimes for none at all. "Just for the hell of it," was Tom's explanation.

Every meal was a veritable "Donegal," with flying and broken dishes the rule rather than the exception. The time Pat Donnelly, at one end of the table and in a rage, flung the baked potato at Robert that flew wide and landed flush on the puss of the guest, McKinnon, Pat was reprimanded by Johannah with the words, "Aim better, Pat!"

There was the occasion when a temporary tranquility came. Johannah, telling McKinnon some story of her youth in the Galty Mountains, became vexed at the numerous interruptions of the rowdy Mike. She solved the problem by suddenly bringing a heavy frying pan down on his head. And she never gave love taps. Mike dozed peacefully on the floor for some minutes, while Johannah went on and finished her story.

Then there was the time when Jennie, accompanied by William on the violin, sang "Kitty Clyde" and "Old Dog Gray." "Jennie had a sweet voice," recalled McKinnon. "But when old Johannah started to sing "Where's Me Other Foot —." Tactfully the sleuth made no further comment on Johannah's vocal endeavors. Perhaps it's just as well.

At first McKinnon could learn little as to any lawless activities of the Donnellys. All of them were suspicious and tight-lipped. Silence was his only answer, when he spoke of having heard of the fires and thefts that occurred in the district. But finally came the break. One night when McKinnon was alone with James Jr. at the latter's house, and the eldest Donnelly boy was well in his cups, he became talkative. Seated on a chair near the kitchen stove, he had been rambling on about this and that, when his gaze went to the sleuth and promptly changed the current subject.

"You — you know, McKinnon, I like you," he told the other. "I liked you ever since I saw how you could handle yourself on the sports field." He drained the contents of his glass and added, a trifle thick-tongued, "but I don't want you to think that you've fooled me or any of the family." He chuckled, pleased with himself, and told, "We're a hard lot to fool."

The sleuth's heart skipped a beat. Damnation — had he somehow, unknowingly, revealed himself? If so, he could sure expect some rough sledding ahead. Now was as good a time as any to find out, so he answered with, "I don't know what you're talking about."

The other laughed. "You're the sly one, McKinnon. Acting the high and mighty gent, and I'll bet if the truth was known, that somewhere the police are looking for you right now."

McKinnon felt relieved but feigned a startled expression. After a pause he answered, "I don't make it a habit to talk about my past."

The reply pleased the eldest son of Jim Donnelly. "Even if you did I'd never repeat it, but a man has to be careful," was his answer. "They hung Tom Jones in London, two years back, for murder, and he'd be alive today if he had had enough sense to keep his mouth shut. As for me, I keep mine shut but I could tell some stories that would raise your hair, if I wanted to."

That was all for awhile, but as the night grew older and drink followed drink, he "wanted to" — at least somewhat. Discretion's barriers lowered by alcohol, he told enough to implicate his brothers, Tom, John, Mike and William, as well as himself in several thefts and arson cases, including the burnings of the Haskett and McMahon barns. Finally on his feet, a garrulous drunk and swaying around the kitchen, "Why do you think everyone around here trembles at the very name of Donnelly?" he went on. "Why do they run like hell at the sight of us? Fear, that's why! And we give 'em all damn good reasons to fear us!''

Boasting, he referred to "the time when I was small enough to walk under a rat's behind with a high silk hat on. I fired the shot into the house that just missed John Farrell. The old man took care of him later and good riddance!''

It was the midnight arrival of William that quieted him. Grim, hard-eyed and suspicious, the gaze of the clubfooted brother went to McKinnon for a lengthy stare, as though aware certain family secrets might have been aired, and he was puzzled as to what should be done about it. Finally, putting the tipsy James to bed and none too gently, he returned to the kitchen and smoked a pipe in silence, his eyes once more on the sleuth in one of those Donnelly glares that made you "hear the sound of shovels digging your grave." At last, hitting his pipe on his palm and still apparently undecided, he returned to the bedroom and sought slumber beside his now snoring brother.

McKinnon spent the remainder of the night on the couch in the kitchen, "with one eye open."

The following morning and "glad to see the sun," McKinnon took his departure and drove straight to Lucan.

He had heard enough to take in at least five of Biddulph's bad boys, and had warrants prepared for the arrest of Mike, Tom, William and James Jr. That would only leave Patrick and Robert, along with old Jim and Johannah, to run at large. The same afternoon, accompanied by a constable and four deputies — all of them armed — McKinnon returned and arrested the five brothers.

All of them were at the old homestead, ready for him, when McKinnon arrived. Evidently he was expected, nor was there any manifested surprise when he announced his identity. James Jr. looked a bit sheepish, though the others were calm enough.

But what surprised McKinnon was the quiet manner in which the five brothers submitted to arrest. Definitely, this was not in accordance with the Black Donnellys. There was no desperate last stand, no kicking or gouging or even a single "you'll never take us alive," utterance. The boys got their hats and coats, seemingly resigned, and went along with the officers. To make the whole thing downright fantastic, Johannah told them to, "Go along peacefully with the gentlemen, boys, and remember what your mother told you." The constable and his deputies gaped at the words. All this — well it just couldn't be! McKinnon was nonplussed.

Of course he had no way of knowing what had been said or planned before his arrival.

But he was to learn, or at least get a pretty good idea, when the day arrived for the five Donnellys to go on trial. Time for the law to exact its pound of flesh, no one, absolutely no one, would appear to press charges against them. Talk about terrorizing a district. McKinnon was chagrined, stalemated as well. He promised protection, he promised everything but the sun, moon and stars, to the would-be prosecutors — No dice. One of them drew him aside and told him, "You may think that all of us are cowards, McKinnon, but it's alright for you. When this is over, you can go back to where you came from. We have to live here — and you don't know the Donnellys!"

Disgusted, McKinnon left the district for the time being.

Mike, Tom, John, William and James Jr., smug and smiling, returned to the homestead and the hearty welcomes of brothers Patrick and Robert, and old Jim and Johannah. Neighbors later told of the wild din that came from the Donnelly farmhouse that night, the celebration in honor of the return of the conquerors. There were many hours of boisterous shouts, peals of laughter and loud stamping of feet, accompanied by the cat-like screechings from the battered fiddle of clubfooted William, as The Devil's Reel, Geese In The Bog and other tunes were wailed out into the night!

CHAPTER SEVEN

They Started Up a Stagecoach Line

They started up a stagecoach line,
And hatred soon was sowed.
Flannigan's rival line, the Donnellys said,
They'd soon drive off the road.

— Old Song

If ever a man was caught in that well-known position, it was on the January night in 1871, when Mike Donnelly attacked, half-killed and robbed big Jim Berryman, on a sideroad just outside of Lucan.

There must have been something unusually loathsome about Berryman's features or something unusually fascinating about his wallet — to a Donnelly. Maybe it was both. Later, Jim Berryman was to receive similar treatment at the hands of brother Tom. Still later he was robbed and beaten a third time by Robert. It became a Donnelly pastime that was sort of routine. However, while Tom and Robert pummeled their victim in comparative seclusion, there were at least three witnesses on the occasion of Mike's all-out attack on Berryman.

Pat "Grouchy" Ryder, a neighbor of the Donnellys and a former friend, who became one of their bitterest enemies, was driving his buggy into Lucan on the night in question, accompanied by two friends, when he saw and recognized Berryman on the road just ahead and making tracks for the village. Ryder laughed and said to the others, "There's 'Big' Jim up ahead and you don't need two guesses to know where he's going — the Old Dominion Bar, I'll bet."

The friends smiled and nodded an understanding. Then the three of them, eyes ahead, saw the one who suddenly sprang from the nearby ditch with a hoarse shout, bounded out onto the road and leaped upon Jim Berryman, fists swinging.

It was burly Mike Donnelly, "drunk and full of the devil." He lashed out with the hard blows that dropped Berryman to his knees, whipped up his boot to the other's jaw in the wicked kick that stretched him out on the road, limp and unconscious, then began a swift search through his victim's clothes. But those in the buggy had seen all; angry shouts arose and Ryder whipped up his horse to bring a speedy rescue. It was not till the three had reached the spot and leaped from the buggy, that they recognized the attacker. Mike Donnelly, noticeably tipsy "and stinking like a distillery," got to his feet with the loot he had obtained, a watch and fourteen dollars.

He frowned, seemingly more annoyed than worried by the presence of the others, before asking: "And just what the hell do you think you can do about it?"

It was the sixty-four dollar question and no one could come up with an answer. What they thought they could do is irrelevant. What they did do was nothing — except stand there like a bunch of gawks. Mike Donnelly, unhindered, took his departure and made his way back to the homesite on lot 18 of the 6th Concession, unworried that his theft had been seen by others. But it was typical of him; Mike Donnelly was usually carefree and indifferent about keeping such matters a secret. Eventually that negligence was to cost him his life and rip cold steel into his back on a Christmas Eve near New Waterford Station.

However, after much delay, Mike Donnelly was arrested for the robbing of Jim Berryman; but taken to court, it was the old story again. No one would appear to testify against him and he had to be released. But given time, luck will eventually run out on everyone. Toronto's The Globe of February 20, 1880, tells of a reporter's interview with a Lucanite, who said of the Donnellys:

"They burned and slashed, and in return we slashed and burned. They got what was coming to them!"

Not much more than a century ago, noticeably around and for some years after The Rebellion of 1837, Canada was sunk in stagnation, poverty and squalor, while just across the border, America was all hustle and progress. In the backwoods townships of the broad Dominion, not more than one in seventy could read. In the Legislative Council that helped control its destiny, many of the members could not read and more could not spell.

But things took a turn for the better with Canada's ever increasing population. Frontiers expanded. Farms and villages came into being, while trees fell before the axes of busy woodsmen. Schools began to appear along sideroads in areas that were formerly bush land. Progress was on the march.

In January 1871, an extra mail train from Lucan to London was established by the Grand Trunk Railway; an Armory and Drill Shed was erected and a hundred inhabitants of the village asked for incorporation. The following year saw the Lucan Council hold its first meeting in Currie's Schoolhouse, and twelve months later the structure was completed that catered so long and faithfully to the needs of the sons of bacchus — the Dublin House.

Ran by short, stout and rollicking Sam Flannery — the spitting image of "Jiggs" in Bringing Up Father, who made it a point to serve five free drinks, "and the best of stuff," to his first twenty-five patrons, every seventeenth of March — the Dublin House became a favorite hang-out of the Donnellys.

The most faithful customer of that emporium of soothing beverages was one Danny Doyle, a local character. Around sixty and about the size of a chew of tobacco, little Danny's anxiety to help the place do business may have accounted for his frequent patronage; but whatever the reason he spent most of his hours there and was the bar's best customer. In fact, usually he was too good a customer. Danny was quiet enough till he got about six noggins under his belt. Then he would have thought nothing of challenging and taking on the combined trio of Tarzan, Superman and Alley Oop.

There came a day when several bad teeth forced Danny to leave his favorite haunt, and journey to a dentist's office in London.

Sober upon entering that house of pain, Danny manifested such nervousness that the dentist suggested he go to the bar downstairs for a drink of "courage". This done and returning to the office, he went so far as to get himself into the dentist's chair. But on seeing the dentist groping among sinister-looking implements, for the second time courage failed Danny. Neither promises nor threats could get him to open his mouth. Finally, impatient and not knowing that John Barleycorn changed Danny from a lamb to a raging lion, the dentist told him to go back downstairs and get a few more drinks to fortify him for the ordeal ahead. Danny was gone about an hour this time, and on his return was just able to navigate.

The dentist asked if he was ready. "Ready? Ready, hell!" answered the diminutive Danny, drawing himself to a fighting stance. "I'd like to see the damn dentist I'd let pull out my teeth now!"

With new settlers steadily coming into the district and the nearby city of London — seventeen miles to the south — ever expanding, by 1872 there were two stagecoach lines operating out of Lucan — the McFee and the Hawkshaw line.

Silver dollars beginning to flow and tinkle throughout the growing Dominion with increasing force, the Donnelly boys decided to cash in on some of them. It resulted in a lull of hostilities for some time; the calm before the storm. William and James Jr. secured jobs driving the McFee stages, with James' farm being run by brother Robert. Patrick obtained employment in London while Mike, "one of the roving kind," began an erratic drifting around the country. That left only Tom and John, along with sister Jennie, on the farm with old Jim and Johannah.

For two years William and James Jr. drove coaches on the Exeter to London run, with Lucan the midway point. Then in May 1873, the two brothers bought out the McFee line.

It was a gala day, that May eighteenth, for the parents as well as the bad boys of Biddulph, when the Donnelly coachline was inaugurated, though enthusiasm seemed to be strictly a family matter. Curiosity, more than anything else, brought the hundred or more who gathered to witness the heralded first run "taking off at noon sharp from the Dublin House." Old Johannah, arrayed in her best finery — some get-up that might have been popular about the time Brian Boroihme beat back the Danes at Clontarf — made one of her rare appearances in Lucan. She embraced her two sons, wished them luck, beamed on the assembly and told them that she hoped they would make it a point to do all their traveling "only in Donnelly coaches."

To make the future seem more promising for the Donnelly brothers, rumor had it that their competitor, "Old Bob" Hawkshaw, planned to retire due to his advanced years. Clubfooted William held the reins for the initial trip of the new coachline into London, with old Jim and Johannah, the guests of honor, for his first two passengers, while the rest of the Donnelly family cheered. No one else did.

Bob Hawkshaw, their competitor, did retire, but not in the manner the Donnelly brothers had hoped he would. Although they offered to buy his horses and coaches, at their price, Hawkshaw sold out to husky John Flannigan, to bring about the beginning of a veritable reign of terror — the longest and the most lawless and barbaric in the annals of Canada.

John Flannigan, around forty at the time he started up his coachline, was a short, powerfully-built man of enormous physical strength, "broad as he was tall", who entertained his friends by bending horseshoes. Born in County Clare, Ireland, he was one of the earliest settlers in the Lucan area, having arrived there with his parents when a boy, twenty-nine years earlier. Naturally, though living on a farm about eight miles from them, he had heard of and known the Donnellys, at least by sight, for the better part of his life "and hated their guts and their bellies for carrying them."

Well liked by the village merchants, as well as the rest of the countryside, Flannigan had every reason to believe that most of the inhabitants of the district would swing their business his way, and there was little to fear from his most unpopular competitors.

There was no cheering from any of the Donnellys at the inauguration of the Flannigan coachline, though the Donnelly glares were evident. As for James Jr. and William, they were anything but secretive regarding their future plans. On the very day their competitor sent his coaches out on their first run, someone went over to the stable of the brothers and mentioned that there wouldn't be a great deal of money for two coachlines in Lucan. The pair smirked; William puffed hard at his pipe for a moment, removed it then grimly announced the words that told precarious days were in the offing:

"There isn't going to be two coachlines in Lucan. You can bet your last dollar, your farm or your very soul on that. Flannigan won't be in business long. We'll drive that horseshoe bending bastard off the road in six months!"

CHAPTER EIGHT

What Happened in Flannigan's Barn

Flannigan found his coaches burned,
Destruction all about.
He'd risen to find his horses splashed with blood —
Their tongues cut out!

— Old Song

Right around the time John Flannigan started his opposition coachline, five months after the opening of the Donnelly line, another unwelcome intrusion entered the lives of the Donnellys. The additional thorn-in-the-side came in the appearance of one Joseph Casswell.

James Donnelly Jr., like his murderous father before him, had settled on acres that did not belong to him; had simply squatted there, asked no questions and regarded the entire matter as a closed book. In his case, however, the land belonged to the Canada Company, who had numerous holdings throughout the territory. Casswell was a stranger to the district, coming from the Niagara area, which undoubtedly explains why he bought land occupied by one of the Donnellys. Most of those who knew them would have shied away from such a deal, as the devil to Holy Water.

But Casswell neither knew the reputation nor had had any dealings with the bad boys of Biddulph. He was soon to learn the former and experience the latter.

James Donnelly's first knowledge that he was to be ousted from his nest came on the October afternoon in 1873, when six men walked into the barn in Lucan, where he and William stabled their horses, and kept their coaches and equipment. William was out on a London-bound coach at the time. Among the six were three Canada Company representatives, as well as Joseph Casswell and Lucan's newest constable. The other man, happening to be passing through the village that very day, had accompanied the others and was an old friend — or — well, at least he was an old acquaintance of James Donnelly, who welcomed a renewal of said acquaintance — Detective Hugh McKinnon.

James Donnelly, inside the barn and greasing a coach-axle, saw the six as they came through the doorway; he stopped his work and came forward, wiping his hands on a dirty rag, an inquiry on his face. Then his eyes fell on the sleuth. "McKinnon. So you're back again, eh? I thought I smelled skunk."

McKinnon was a tactful as well as brave man. The words brought only a smile. "So you remember me?" he asked.

"Remember you? I'd remember your dirty hide on a bush," was James Donnelly's answer. "You had a lot of trouble for nothing, the last time, didn't you? You put me and four of my brothers — five innocent men — before a judge." His eyes narrowed; the rag dropped from the hands he clenched into fists. It was evident he was struggling with himself to keep from crashing them into McKinnon's face.

"You did your damnedest, you with your sneaky methods, to put us behind bars for as long as you could," he went on, his voice rising. "It would have been for keeps, if you had your way. But you didn't; you weren't able to make any of the charges stick. And now you're back. What's it this time; out to raise some more stink?"

McKinnon replied he was there to tell him that the acres he had settled on — land legally owned for quite some time by the Canada Company — had been purchased by Joseph Casswell, who intended to take immediate possession and had every right to do so. Of course, several times in the past, representatives of the Canada Company had driven out to the farmhouse of James Donnelly, told him the land was not his and ordered him to vacate. But he had dismissed it all with a laugh, and a "get-to-hell-out-of-here" to the representative.

Now, however, things were different. The land had been sold and the Canada Company meant to evict him from the property to make way for the rightful owner.

They had the law behind them and would bring in any outside help needed to enforce it. McKinnon emphasized that adding, "And if any harm befalls either Mr. Casswell or his property — I just happened to be passing through Lucan on Government business — I'll come back, 'Johnny-on-the-spot,' and I'll know just who to arrest."

"Another word out of you, McKinnon, and you won't leave here, let alone come back. I'll beat your damn brains out!"

The six men left the barn with McKinnon's brains still intact. James Donnelly promptly took the matter to court, claiming squatter's rights. But the orders he had received to evacuate the property didn't give him the proverbial leg to stand on and judgment went against him. But the Canada Company was fair and, though under no obligation, compensated him somewhat for his loss. He left the courtroom, vowing vengeance and cursing Casswell and his ancestors as far back as the flood. None of his listeners reminded him that the land had not been his in the first place. They knew better. Along with William, James Donnelly returned to the house of his father — and made plans.

So poor, misguided Joseph Casswell, along with his wife and two children, moved on to his newly acquired acres, hoping for a long and prosperous life in a new and prosperous country. The illusion was soon broken. On the morning of the fourth day after taking possession of the land, he discovered that during the night, vandals had entered his barn and disemboweled his horses. It was a gory sight, given a macabre emphasis by the mutilated body of the farm collie hanging from a rafter.

Before the month had elapsed, the throats of more than half of Casswell's cows had been cut, his buggy, cutter and wagons sawed apart. There was the night when the Casswells were awakened to find their home in flames and were barely able to escape from it with their lives. Striking with the stealth of shadows, Casswell was unable to see or prove the identity of the fiendish destroyers, who left a note informing, "This is only the beginning."

It was only the beginning for Joseph Casswell who had, through no fault of his own become the target and plaything of the most vicious and heartless bunch of devils that ever drew the breath of human life.

The following spring, Casswell's newly erected barns and outhouses mysteriously went up in flames one night. But this time the arsonists left tracks — hoof tracks — in a light snow that had fallen after midnight. Casswell and his wife took up the trail. Traced for five miles, the tracks led directly to the Donnelly farmhouse. It was enough for Casswell; he hurried into Lucan and brought charges against the Donnellys. But once more history repeated itself. Taken before a judge, there was not enough proof to convict them and again Biddulph's bad boys were released, despite the protests of Casswell and Detective McKinnon, who had hurried to Lucan.

After the trial the sleuth was warned by William Donnelly, "Listen stupid! One of these fine days you are going to stick that ugly thing that you call your face into our affairs once too often. Then you won't have a face!"

The following month, returning to his home after a night in Lucan, Casswell unexpectedly met Robert Donnelly on the Roman Line. The eyes of Donnelly widened and lit, in the manner of one unable to believe his good fortune, when he recognized the other. "Well, well, well!" exclaimed Robert Donnelly. "The one man I wanted most in the world to meet, and here we are alone. God is good and the devil isn't too bad either!" Robert Donnelly then gave Casswell a merciless beating, breaking his arm, his jaw, several ribs, closing both eyes and leaving him for dead.

After two weeks in bed, Casswell again went to the authorities in Lucan. He was told to, "forget it and be glad you're still alive!"

Desperate, Casswell carried on as best he could throughout a summer marked by further mutilation to three new horses he had purchased. He found the fire made of fence rails surrounding his reaping machine that destroyed it. He was unable to get the thrashers he needed to help him with his crops, as everyone was afraid to aid him, fearing Donnelly retaliation. Four of his cows were poisoned, his buggy and wagons again sawed apart.

Then came the Christmas night when the sleeping Casswell family, for the second time, was awakened and had to flee, hastily clad, from their blazing home into the bitter December cold. Nearby, the barn and outhouses again flared to destruction; everything a mass of flames. From the roadway Casswell saw the five masked riders, who shouted that he and his family would, "either get to hell out of the country or be carried to the graveyard — food for the worms!"

Then the five rode off, wild yells of triumph mingling with galloping hooves and the sky behind them a swirling orange glow, while the Casswells watched their world crumble to ashes around them.

Once more tracks were found in the snow. Once more they were followed and led directly to — yes, you guessed it — the Donnelly farmhouse. But proving that Biddulph's bad boys had anything to do with the fires — well, it just couldn't be done. In after years Casswell told, "Despite the mask and the hat pulled down low on her head, I recognized her, and I'd be willing to swear that one of those five riders that night was the old woman herself Johannah!"

Ruined, Joseph Casswell could not keep up the payments on his farm, lost it and left the district, to take up quarters in a tenement house in London. He had it plenty tough for some years. It can be understood why he told a reporter, after hearing of the Donnelly massacre, "Hurrah! Wiping out those wild dogs was the best thing that could have happened to Canada, outside of smothering them at birth! I'm going out and celebrate, and I'll bet there are hundreds of others doing the same thing!"

There were!

William and James Donnelly, out to make good their boast, that they would drive John Flannigan, "that horse-shoe bending bastard," off the road in six months, started their war against their competitor with a price cut, a drastic reduction in rates.

Their plans boomeranged on them. Far from showing any fear or being forced into bankruptcy by the lowered rates, Flannigan met the cut then launched a price war of his own that soon had both coachlines operating at a loss. Eventual ruin threatened the Donnelly Line; they couldn't carry on as long as their competitor. The brothers had only their own and old Jim's capital to work on. Not a great deal to say the least. On the other hand, Flannigan had some money and scores of friends and acquaintances, including every merchant and business man in Lucan, who would go to any length to see him win over the hated Donnellys.

The result was inevitable; most of the populace threw all their business to Flannigan, and the Donnelly coaches began going out empty.

In time, even in London, William and James Donnelly found their coachline boycotted. There was little they could do about it; nothing, in fact. Along with the stories that had come out of Lucan, stories telling of the lawlessness and violence that prevailed in the area, London had heard the names of those said to be responsible for it all; names that were becoming notorious, even in districts a day and two days drive away by coach. To give the brothers credit, they had set up a fast-driving line and kept to a rigid schedule. Neither rain nor snow stopped the Donnelly coaches, with the informative, blue-painted words just above the doors, "We Get You There."

But William and James Donnelly could not silence the ever-increasing number of stories told about them or the family. Even then, in Lucan as well as its surrounding villages of Granton, Centralia, Elginfield and Exeter, mothers were silencing unruly children with the dire threat, "Hush — or the Black Donnellys will get you!" And there was that parody on a nursery rhyme that many a London youngster was chanting:

"How many miles to London Town?
Three score and ten, Sir.
I've just come in by Donnelly coach.
Then you're as bad as them, Sir."

In brief, the late summer of 1875 found the Donnelly stagecoach line on its last legs, groggy and ready to hit the canvas. Certainly the reputation of Biddulph's bad boys had not been enhanced since the beginning of the year.

Mike Donnelly, again beneath the family roof, after months of travel and sleeping in the better haymows, had been accused of stealing and selling a horse near Ailsa Craig. Old Jim and Johannah had just been freed from an arson charge, but doubts still lingered as to their innocence. In London, Robert was being imputed for slugging and robbing two drunks; and in his home village Tom had upheld the family name by beating up the latest Lucan constable, who had resigned his commission. The village fathers were looking for another human punching bag for Donnelly fists.

Again, there was the case of Thompson's Harness Shop. Thompson was a known enemy of the Donnellys — four years later one of his cows was instrumental in bringing around their downfall — and on a night in March 1875, Thompson's Harness Shop had been destroyed by fire. The usual rumors had made the rounds: "The work of the Black Donnellys! Up to their old tricks again!" However, the origin of the fire was never determined for a certainty; yet its occurrence had not added any prestige to the Donnelly name nor caused patrons to flock to the coaches of William and James.

August found the chips down and the business of the two brothers steadily gliding up that well-known creek. But an old saying tells, "There's more than one way to skin a cat." Late on the night of August 23, while the village of Lucan slept, several men slunk quietly through the blackness and made their way to John Flannigan's barn.

Early the following morning Flannigan came to the barn for the first hitch-up to London. A grim sight met his eyes; carnage was everywhere. His two coaches had been sawed apart, his harness and other equipment slashed to bits and strewn around. The stalls of his horses were splashed with blood, its smell was heavy in the air; while the poor beasts themselves, having broken their halter ropes, were pawing the ground and running frenziedly around the barn, crazed with agony as well they might have been.

For during the night their tongues had been cut out!

CHAPTER NINE

When Hell Broke Loose

With fists and clubs they fought the Donnellys,
Under moon and sun.
In village streets and on sideroads —
Ah, but the Donnellys always won.
— Old Song

In the fall of 1874, Jennie Donnelly, nineteen at the time, had first met the young man who won her heart. Cupid's dart struck deep while she was visiting relatives in St. Thomas, who had invited friends to the house "to meet our pretty cousin from Lucan."

Jennie's shyness, quick blushes and wide, deep-blue eyes, caused the heart of one young man, the son of a well-to-do merchant and landowner, to beat faster. By all accounts, she had an unusual voice, "like the tinkle of chimes," and her lovely renditions of "The Garden Where The Praties Grow, Father O'Flynn, Colleen Malone" and other airs from the auld sod, must have made the conquest complete. She returned to the family, but a short while later found him a visitor at the farm, where he won the so hard to win approval of the Donnelly family. Johannah proclaimed him, "A foin broth of a boy."

The following summer, Jennie and her young man were married and settled in St. Thomas, where they prospered, raised a family of four, lived a long and happy life, and were respected and numbered among the leading citizens of the community.

There is little more to be told of Jennie Donnelly. At this point she drifts out of our story, as quiet and inconspicuous as was her presence in it. There is not a great deal to be learned of her, other than she was a very pretty girl who, until the time she went to St. Thomas, seldom left the Donnelly acres and was rarely seen, even by the neighboring farmers. The Globe makes a brief mention of her, however, telling of her attending the funeral of her murdered parents and brothers, acompanied by her husband and three small children; and of her "gazing at the coffins with tearfilled eyes." So barbaric had been the massacre, the bodies of four of the battered, slashed and burned Donnellys, were buried in one casket.

Jennie is recorded having said, "John was my favorite brother." At the time of the killings, it was well known that the murder of John Donnelly was a case of mistaken identity. Fate had him open the wrong door at the wrong moment. The thirty or more slugs that almost tore John Donnelly apart, sprawling him on his face in a February snow, were meant for "that clubfooted devil of a William!"

John Flannigan discovered the atrocities that had occured in his barn on the night of August 23, 1875, around six a.m. on the following morning when he went there to harness up for the first trip to London. The horses, tongueless and crazed with agony, were dashing about in terror. At the sight, Flannigan nearly went crazy himself. A rumble of wheels caused him to turn. John Purtell, a slender built, insignificant and somewhat feeble-minded farmhand, had driven a light milk cart into Lucan early that morning to pick up several bags of meal for his employer. Purtell was later to be one of the six who went on trial, charged with being the ringleaders of the mob that massacred the Donnellys. John Purtell was the first to learn of the outrage. As he drove the milk cart by the barn, Flannigan roared.

"I had visitors last night — the Black Donnellys! Come over here, Purtell and see what happened. Come over here and see what those bastards did! By God I'll have the hide of everyone of them for this, and bury them in a manure pile!"

Purtell brought the cart to a sharp halt, leaped off it, and the next moment was beside him, wide eyed and speechless.

John Flannigan secured a shotgun and a box of shells from the small, locked room he used as an office. He had been in the habit of taking the gun with him on his daily trips, for the past several months, just in the event he ran into some trouble with the Donnellys. Now he found he had plenty of it on his hands. Cursing a blue streak he readied himself for the first step, to handle the immediate problem. Revenge could wait for a few minutes. Shotgun in hand, one by one, he put his horses out of their misery — the gun reports roaring loudly in the morning silence of the village.

In the rather dim light of the barn's interior and with the horses running back and forth in crazed confusion, it took him the better part of a half-hour to do the job. By that time Flannigan was primed to, as he shouted, "kill the whole damn Donnelly family."

After that one look into the barn, John Purtell had gone tearing up the street in the milk cart, shouting out the news to the awakening village in the manner of Paul Revere warning of the oncoming Redcoats. It was a big day of importance in the life of the hardly ever noticed farmhand. After traversing the main street, he sent his charger plunging down the side ones, the light milk cart bouncing and careening around corners as he kept shouting, "Get over to the Flannigan barn — all hell has broke loose!"

Windows and doors opened; villagers came streaming from their homes. It wasn't long before a small crowd had gathered before the barn — the continuous shots from within an added magnet of attraction. A few of the bolder men went inside the barn, and what they saw and reported to the others made it evident that drastic measures were in the immediate offing. In no time everyone knew what had happened. None seemed to question or doubt the identity of the vandals who had done the grisly work. To all of them the name was evident as though each had witnessed the atrocity.

"The Black Donnellys, of course. Who else but a Donnelly would do anything like this?" Then threats were heard, while work-hardened fists were clenched and faces became grim. This time the Donnellys had gone too far!

By the time Flannigan, splashed with blood and perspiring, had finished his task and walked from the barn into the morning sunlight, at least a hundred of the villagers were before him. To be sure, many of them were women, chittering and curious, and more than one Lucan youngster had left the morning chores unfinished, to hurry over to the barn. But among those present were men who had hated the Donnellys for years. And now this —.

A few fiery words and a capable leader, and they would be ready for anything.

Standing before them John Flannigan, breathing hard, blew smoke from the barrels of his gun, then loaded it in the slow, emphatic manner that told his intentions. Mike

Molony, who ran the local wagonshop, was among the gathering. He spoke up. "It's an outrage, John! A vile, inhuman outrage! We should drive everyone of them out of the country!" Someone shouted, "We should hang them!"

But threats didn't interest John Flannigan. He was out for action — immediate, violent and on a mass scale. Eyes flashing, his thick red hair disheveled, "Who's coming with me?" he demanded. "You all know what happened; you all know who did it. They've terrorized this district for years, and caused families to leave it, but this is the pay-off. Let them get away with this and they'll be coming into our houses next, slitting our throats while we sleep!"

"What do you want us to do, John?" asked Molony.

"Just what you think you should do," was the answer. "You women and youngsters get back to your homes and stay there," ordered Flannigan. "As for you men, I'm not telling you what to do; it's up to you. But I know what I'm going to do; I'm going over to the Donnelly barn right now, and I'm taking this gun with me. Any of you that have an ounce of guts will come along. The rest — I don't want."

John Flannigan, scowling, broad and determined, pushed his way through the crowd and reached the road. The gun at hip level, he began a steady advance towards the Donnelly barn — a grim picture of Canadian pioneer vengeance. Before he had gone twenty paces there were seventeen men at his heels, nearly all of them hastily armed with clubs, though a few carried the shotguns they had brought with them from their homes. One practical and far-sighted man carried a rope.

A score of others followed the marchers from the comparative safety of the board sidewalks — cautious and curious individuals who wished to see all, but take no part in the impending battle.

When John Flannigan and his seventeen supporters drew near the Donnelly barn, they could see William and James Jr. with the coach that was about to depart for the morning run to London. The brothers had been making it a practice, for some months, to send out the first stage at 6:45 a.m., fifteen minutes before their competitor swung into the day's activities. The early departure of their stage was responsible for some business.

Inside the coach and ready to be off, were three passengers, a farm implements salesman and two women. One of the latter was destined to live to an unusual age. In later life she settled in British Columbia and before her death related the story of that wild morning to some scribe, who eventually wrote an article on it.

The two brothers were seemingly unaware of the oncoming mob at first, though later events proved this was anything but the case.

William Donnelly was busying himself with lifting the baggage of his passengers into a box at the rear of the coach, while James removed the halter snap at the lead horse tied to the hitching rail. As the men came closer, it was James who apparently first noticed them. He pointed to them and shouted the three words to his brother, "We have visitors!" A close observation would have revealed that neither William nor James Donnelly wore coats, and the shirtsleeves of both were rolled up as though each was expecting to be called upon for some strenuous physical task.

James left the horses and joined his brother as they walked out onto the road to await the oncoming men, each carrying a stout club. William Donnelly, a pace or so ahead of his brother, turned in the roadway and called out to his passengers: "Stay in your seats, folks, this won't take long. The coach will be pulling out on time!"

The words didn't seem to make much sense to the passengers or anyone else — just then. After all, two men against eighteen.

The kill-crazed Flannigan, shotgun still clutched in his big hands, walked relentlessly on, those behind him following closely. The fact that the two brothers had obviously been expecting him and were ready to fight, didn't deter the other. But then, probably nothing would have. Flannigan was out for blood and meant to have it. As he drew nearer it became apparent that he had but one purpose in mind; to walk right up to William Donnelly, ram the gun deep into his belly and pull the trigger — possibly both of them. With Flannigan less than a dozen paces from him, William raised himself slightly on his toes in a tensed position; his eyes narrowed, the club at his side began to swing back and forth — jerkedly.

From the nearby sidewalks the less courageous Lucanites watched — and waited. This was it, something they would be telling to future grandchildren!

Then, with Flannigan not ten paces from William, a drawn-out, blood-curdling yell stabbed out of the Donnelly barn and broke the tense silence. The next minute, old Jim Donnelly, returning to the wars, walked out of the barn with the quick movements of former days that belied his fifty-nine years. Behind him came his five other sons — Robert, John, Mike, Tom and Patrick. The latter had been working in London, but the previous evening saw his return to the home roost. Perhaps the family, realizing his services would soon be needed, had sent for him. Anyhow, his arrival was most timely — for them.

Imitating William and James Jr., all of the boys as well as old Jim, had discarded their coats and rolled up their shirt sleeves. And everyone of them carried a sturdy club, weapons the use of which they had perfected about the time the average youngster is shooting marbles.

At the unexpected appearance of six more Donnellys, Flannigan and his followers came to a halt. This was a surprise! So the Black Donnellys had it all planned out and were ready for them, eh? Even as Flannigan must have thought this, old Jim and the others walked up to and were beside William and James Jr. Now, united in full force, they were ready to get started, despite the heavy odds. This was evident by old Jim's first words to the mob:

"You gentlemen seem to be looking for trouble. If so, the boys and I will be pleased to oblige you!"

There was a pause as the two forces faced each other, in the early sunrays of that August morning. Eight on one side, eighteen on the other. All of the Donnelly boys, smiling and fearless, close to the six-foot mark, well-built and undeniably handsome — even their enemies admitted that — with the swarthy, well-chiseled features and thick, wavy black hair that distinguished each of them, seemed to welcome the situation. They threw several taunts at the enemy and William called out, "Why the delay — let's get started!" It brought a ripple of laughter from the ranks of the bad boys of Biddulph.

The unexpected developments seemed to puzzle John Flannigan. To be sure, he and his followers represented pioneer justice and retaliation. They were there in a worthy cause, while the Black Donnellys represented only — the Black Donnellys. But Flannigan had apparently been intent on killing William Donnelly. Now, with old Jim directly before him, laughing in his face, it was hard for him to adjust himself to the altered circumstances. But slowly the gun swung from the son to the father. Then with a shout, Flannigan flung it to his shoulder. He was not fast enough.

Old Jim Donnelly slid under the gun-barrel, grasped it with his two hands and tore it from Flannigan's grasp, then rammed the butt hard into the face of his foe. Blood shot forth. As Flannigan fell back, hands to his smashed face, old Jim swung the gun over his head and brought it down on Flannigan's skull, with a force that caused the wooden butt to fly asunder!

Then all hell broke loose!

Remember what Detective McKinnon said of the Donnellys? "When fighting they became as howling maniacs, resembling nothing human, while snarling, clawing and biting with the fury of wild beasts at bay!"

Even as the gun-butt was being brought down on Flannigan's head, the bad boys of Biddulph had gone into action, plowing into their enemies with an utter disregard of life and limb, and a savagery that was appalling. John Purtell, the milk cart Paul Revere, ran into grief right at the start; his period of service in the combat can be numbered in seconds. Fate placed Purtell directly before Tom Donnelly, who singled out the farmhand for victim number one, knocked the club from his hand then brought his own over in a vicious backhand sweep that laid Purtell out, cold. It was only a sample of what Tom Donnelly had in store for his enemies. They found that out as he fought his way among them, twisting, dodging, sidestepping — seemingly in two places at once — with his club lashing out right and left.

His brothers surged forward, battling with an equal fury and taking the offensive, while keeping up a series of wild yells that quailed the hearts of Flannigan's followers. With the battle less than a minute old, several members of the mob had already been clubbed to their knees and were screaming for quarter; appeals that were practically drowned out in the frenzied din and would have gone unheeded anyhow.

Mike Donnelly's vicious attack on two Flannigan men finally forced them to give ground before the rain of club-blows coming their way, then turn and run into an adjacent blacksmith shop. Mike, bounding at their heels and keeping up his war cries, followed them there, ignored their pleas for mercy, clubbed both unconscious then returned to the fray, seeking other conquests.

Several of the men in the mob had carried shotguns. But they never used them, and for the very good reason that they never had the chance. Shooting was made difficult with their friends intermingling with their enemies in surging masses and the armed men had been singled out and were among the first to fall beneath Donnelly clubs. Old Jim obtained, then unloaded three shotguns and threw them well out of the range of combat, exclaiming, "Weapons of the weak — fit only for cowards!" The Donnellys rarely employed guns with the exception of Robert, who was later sent to the penitentiary as the result of using Lucan's Constable Everett for target practice.

Meanwhile the spectators on the sidewalks were getting the thrill of a lifetime, and material for five generations of tall-tales swapping. As for law enforcement — there was none. Who knows, maybe the Lucan constable was sitting up with a sick friend? It is certain he made no public appearance.

It is not known which one of Biddulph's bad boys bit off the nose of one member of the mob; but it was Robert who picked up another, raised him to arms length and pitched him headlong through a store window. Having lost his club, Patrick Donnelly hurried to the blacksmith shop and returned with the horseshoes he sent sailing at his foes

— iron discs of destruction. James Jr. and John won meritorious acclaim for their feats on the field of combat that day; and Old Jim Donnelly finally had the satisfaction of meeting up with and downing "Grouchy" Ryder, his neighbor for more than two decades, in a fast and furious melee. "Praise that moment!" he afterwards voiced. "My hands had been itchin' to tan old 'Grouchy's' hide for twenty years!"

William raised hell with that clubfoot of his, on the face of more than one downed foe. Trust fiddling Billy to do that!

Briefly, it can all be summed up with the indisputable truth that the Donnellys were the masters that day and their foes never had a chance, despite the better than two-to-one odds. In less than ten minutes from the time Flannigan went down, his supporters were in full flight, tearing down the road and being pursued by old Jim's wild brood. But even before the ending, the sidewalk spectators, realizing the inevitable outcome, were hurrying towards their homes with the utter lack of dignity that caused several falls, turned ankles, bruises and other minor casualties.

It was during the retreat that an utterance was spoken which was to be quoted and requoted in following years. "Let's walk home, Henry," a frightened housewife said to her husband, seeing the departure of the others and wanting the safety of her four walls. "Walk, hell, let's run, Mariah," was the answer of her none too courageous spouse. "Walk, hell, let's run, Mariah!" became a popular expression throughout the district.

With the enemy departed, the streets deserted and the Donnellys unquestioned possessors of their surroundings, William returned to the stage and his three passengers. Chalk-white, the trio had been but gaping, mute spectators. With the danger over, however, the women began to scream, screams that continued to rise till they reached air-raid siren proportions. William's efforts to quieten them failed. Shouting to one of them, "For God's sake, Madam, shut up — I could have triplets with less fuss than that," William Donnelly leaped up to the driver's seat and got the coach under way, ignoring the screams and protests of his passengers. They had bought fares to London and that is where he took them.

The Donnelly coach went out on time!

John Flannigan proved to have a harder head than the deceased Farrell. When he eventually came to himself, he sat up, splashed with crimson, and after a few minutes was able to gain his feet and stagger away under his own power. Of course he had little choice; there were none of his friends around to help him. The Donnellys were near-by, but he could expect little assistance from them.

The shouts and taunts of the victors reached his ears, as Flannigan made his slow and dismal, one-man retreat back to his barn.

Joy reigned in the camp of the enemy; not one of them carried as much as a scratch. Old Jim and his sons remained in the village for the balance of the day, each of them relating his personal accomplishments in the victory. Laughing and jubilant, they paraded up and down the streets, daring anyone, including the law, to come out and fight. No one appeared. The sick friend of the Lucan constable must have been near death's door.

Of course the big loser of the day was John Flannigan. He realized he would have to begin practically all over again. His horses had had to be destroyed, his coaches were useless. But with him out of business, the Donnellys would have a full and unchallenged run of the road, with all the gravy coming their way. By all the snakes St.

Patrick drove out of Ireland, he wasn't going to stand for
that! Flannigan showed admirable spirit. Within forty-
eight hours he was negotiating for new horses and two
stages in London. Seven days after discovering the atrocity
in his barn, he was ready to resume operations, the first
run scheduled for 7 a.m. on the following morning. It was
a schedule that was never carried out.

Around 2 a.m. on the morning of September 1, seven
men again slunk quietly through the darkness and made
their way to Flannigan's barn. A short while later, a flaming holocaust, it crumbled to the ground!

CHAPTER TEN

Fire and More Fires

The countryside became a place
That lived in fear of night.
When burning barns and fields would flame
The heavens with their light.

— Old Song

Even today, around Lucan, Ontario, you find the pro-Donnelly and anti-Donnelly groups. The thirty-three-year-old Donnelly feud has never ceased being hotly debated since its murderous climax on the morning of February 4, 1880. While those murders were being discussed at a meeting of the Middlesex Historical Society at London, Ontario, an elderly man strode angrily from the room, then paused in a doorway to shout:

"The Donnellys might have cut the tongues out of men, but never out of horses!"

But another old boy with a good eighty winters on him, rose from a chair to wave his cane and retort: "You're a damn liar and you know it! The Donnellys were murdering devils, every one of them. Look what they did to my own father!"

And Lucan's constable, big Dave Egan, ever on the lookout for trouble — especially on Saturday nights, when

93

the surrounding farmers drive into the village for supplies and to "hoist a few" — will tell you: "It's like someone was playing a piano. He goes along alright for awhile, then strikes the wrong note." That "wrong note" is any ill-timed mention of the Donnelly feud.

For despite their many unquestioned depravities, the barbaric manner of the massacre of the Donnellys and the passing of years has aroused sympathy in many. There are those who will tell you that the continuous persecutions of their enemies — "hangdogs" — as well as the law, were responsible for the transgressions of Biddulph's bad boys. Old records and newspapers, however, do not verify that "more sinned against than sinned," theory.

Travel some day up Lucan way, and go out on the Roman Line. There you will find the clock of time has seemingly turned its hands back.

Finding the road that knew the violence of the Donnellys will not be difficult. Leaving London, Ontario and driving north on Richmond Street, once you are beyond the city's limits you will see some of the land that has made Canada famous; flat and fertile territory, the Mecca of the agriculturist. You will pass a crossroad, about ten miles from London, that is grimly linked with the past. According to one story, scarcely forty yards on the right from the highway, Tom Donnelly once held the hand of a male schoolteacher, while Mike bent the pedagog's fingers back and snapped them, one by one, like chalk.

It was down this same sideroad that James Jr. was riding, following his robbery of the Granton Post Office, when he was overtaken by a posse of three. Pulled from his horse, Jim Donnelly's eldest son, after a furious struggle, laid out his pursuers, rode on and finally made his way to the border and Detroit, where he remained in hiding for several months.

Your mileage gauge should clock fourteen miles and decimal two, after leaving London and traveling a broad highway, every inch of which has known the rumble of Donnelly coaches, when you reach Elginfield. Of course if some cow, out for its morning constitutional, happens to stroll along she will blot out the sight of the village, so look sharp and don't blink or you will miss the place. Some of the oldtimers of Elginfield can tell you grim tales of the Donnellys. Two miles further on you will come to St. Patrick's Church and the Roman Line.

A turn to the right will put you on it and in front of the church — and the graveyard.

At once you will be struck by the tomb-like stillness, an air of mournful solitude that makes a sneeze sound as a desecration. Somehow you will get the eerie feeling that you have suddenly stepped backward into time and nowhere in the world is the silence so silent as out on the Roman Line — especially after midnight.

In the churchyard you will find the graves of many who experienced the entire Donnelly feud, and fought against Biddulph's bad boys for years. Some of the headstones date back well over a century. The unfortunate John Farrell is buried there, also James Carroll, "The only man who didn't fear the Black Donnellys," as well as others who helped to comprise the mob in that last raid on the Donnelly farmhouse. At the far end of the churchyard you will find the Donnelly plot, and the inscriptions that tell its inmates were "MURDERED."

William Donnelly and his wife are buried there, as well as Mike, old Jim and Johannah, James Jr., John, Tom and a niece, Bridget, who had arrived at the Donnelly farmhouse from Tipperary, Ireland — a weak-minded girl — only a short while before she fell beneath the clubs of the mob.

Of course you will want to see the old Donnelly farm. It's three miles up the road, on the left side and you can't miss it. Drive slowly and take in the sights, although you won't see much other than flat areas of countryside, a few crossroads and the occasional farmhouse, some of them deserted and their bare upper windows appearing as watching eyes. But you are now in the heart of the country that knew the violence and depravities of the Donnelly feud and — as one Pat Whalen later testified — "so many cases of poisoned cattle, mutilations and fires that we lost track of them. There was a time, when the night skies weren't lit with flame was the exception."

Three hundred yards before reaching the old Donnelly place, and on the left side of the road, you will pass the lamppost ready to topple and long deserted farmhouse of John Farrell — the one he was working so hurriedly to erect, when he explained his tireless energy to his helpers with the words, "Every time I sink an axe into wood I keep wishin' it was that damn Donnelly's head!"

The log house that was the home of the Donnellys — it was rebuilt once after being burned down by their enemies — was originally erected away back in 1847, and not ten paces from where the present farmhouse now stands. What tales that strip of land might tell if it had a tongue. Today, while starlings dive, chirp and soar in the blueness overhead, and cattle graze in surrounding fields, only a growth of long grass, several old and discarded wagon wheels, and a few bits of lumber mark the site where once stood the house built by Jim and Johannah Donnelly.

There they lived for almost thirty-three years and raised their family; there they plotted, ordered and directed the atrocities that kept the countryside in a reign of terror. And there, along with their sons, they were finally clubbed to death and burned, in the massacre still referred to as the blackest crime ever committed in Canada.

There is nothing to suggest the hectic bygone years the place once knew. No hostile mobs advance upon the farm today. A short distance behind the present barn, the once heavily wooded area where Jim Donnelly hid from the law has long fallen before the axes of progress. Of course the fields are still there, the same fields he worked "dressed in a woman's clothes."

In the distance can be seen the buildings of the Ryder farm. Old Jim and Johannah Donnelly were scheduled to appear in the Granton court, charged with burning the Ryder barn, on the very morning they were murdered.

Yes, on the night of September 1, 1875, and just a little more than a week after his horses had been mutilated, the barn of John Flannigan had been destroyed by arsonists.

The following morning, when the news of the fire became known, again all hell threatened, with Lucan apparently to become a battlefield for the second time in eight days. No store opened in Lucan that day; few if anyone walked its streets and most of the houses remained locked, with tension fairly crackling the air. Numerous farmers from the surrounding districts, however, who had seen the blazing sky in the previous night and guessed the rest, arrived by roundabout trails and made their way to the still-smoking embers that had been Flannigan's barn at the south end of the village.

The only other signs of life were the forms moving in and out of the Donnelly barn, at the far end of the street. It was noticed, although old Jim had recently characterized guns as weapons fit only for the weak, that for the first time in the memory of the oldest inhabitant, Biddulph's bad boys had armed themselves. That was apparent when three curious farmers approached the barn. Mike and Tom

Donnelly, both carrying shotguns, walked out onto the road, and the latter shouted out to the trio:

"Get back there where you belong, with Flannigan and the other rats, or we'll spread your guts all over the road!"

The three retreated.

When William, accompanied by John finally drove the Donnelly stage — London bound — out of Lucan that morning, both of them sat in the driver's seat with a shotgun across their knees. The coach's only occupant, old Jim, carried and exhibited his trusty club. When the stage came abreast of the ruins that had been Flannigan's barn, Mike Stanley, a farmer, led several of the men assembled there in a half-hearted attempt to halt it. But they fell back when John fired one of the barrels of his gun over their heads.

Old Jim, his head, shoulders and club protruding from the coach door, had seen all. He gave Stanley one of his "Donnelly glares" as the coach rolled by, and called out: "I'll remember this, Mike Stanley, and I'll give you a damn good reason to!"

At the Donnelly barn, the other brothers took turns at sentry duty for the remainder of the day.

John Flannigan surprised everyone that day by doing nothing. But the old story of, "It wasn't what he did, it was the way he did it," told the others he had no intention of calling quits. Only this time he did not storm and howl for Donnelly blood. Flannigan, who had been able to save both his horses and coaches before the barn collapsed, looked grim but said little. He seemed to be thinking — thinking — and paid scant attention to those around him. When someone suggested another attack on the fortress of his enemy, his only answer was a headshake. Around noon he told them all to return to their homes, adding:

"Don't worry, men, the Donnellys haven't heard the last of this. But the sun will rise tomorrow, the day after and the next day too, and from now on I'm fighting fire with fire — and mine will be the hottest!"

That night Mike Stanley, the farmer who had attempted to stop the Donnelly coach, had a good reason to recall the threat of old Jim. Five masked men broke down the door of his farmhouse as he slept, and dragged Stanley from his bed, while the frightened shrieks of his wife went octaves above high C. Told, "Maybe this will learn you to stay in line," Stanley was hurried into the yard, tied to a tree and horsewhipped till he blacked out. When he came to himself, his wife was bending over him, the masked men had ridden off and his barn was flaming to destruction. His horses had been hamstrung.

Although he had recognized the voices of the five men responsible for the despicable outrage, Mike Stanley never brought charges against them. After all, he still had his life, his wife and his house; and he had heard grim stories of what happened to informers!

So for awhile, Flannigan out of business, temporarily at least, the Donnelly coachline had the sole run of the road. It was a golden opportunity in an ever-increasing and thriving district, and William and James Jr. made the most of it. With welcomed dollars flowing into their coffers they promptly raised the rate tarriff, bought and put two more coaches on the road, increased their London schedule to three runs a day and made an additional daily trip to Exeter. There they used the lobby of the Central Hotel for their terminal. There they met the local man who contemplated the starting of a rival coachline. The brothers warned that such a venture for him, would provide "a one-way ticket to hell!"

Brothers Mike and Robert were added to the staff of the Donnelly coachline in the capacity of drivers, with Tom substituting on occasions.

Several times, with business extra brisk, old Jim himself took a turn at the reins and on one trip, when the stork overtook an expectant mother who was being hurried to London, he performed the duties of a midwife in the coach and helped to bring a baby boy, alive and kicking, into the world.

If he ever did any other good turn in his life, it has not been recorded.

For six weeks the Donnelly stages rumbled on without opposition. Then came another night when men slunk through the darkness of sleeping Lucan, and towards the barn that was set aflame and burned to the ground. The following morning the entire countryside was aware of the latest destruction, but this time there was rejoicing instead of anger; for the structure that went up in flames that night was the barn that belonged to the Donnellys.

Three of their horses and two coaches were lost in the fire, along with harness and equipment.

William and James promptly brought action against John Flannigan, charging arson. They swore he had been seen in the vicinity of the barn minutes before the fire occurred. But as the defense bluntly put it, "No one would believe a Donnelly even under oath." The brothers, William raging and stamping his clubfoot, were practically laughed out of court. Flannigan had an airtight alibi; on the night of the fire and for two days before that time, he had been more than a hundred miles away, at the farm of a sister who lived near a crossroads settlement that rejoiced in the name of Punkeydoodle's Corners. Strum that one on your zither.

Both coachlines at a standstill, it became a race as to which would be first to resume operation. Time was the important factor. Here, however, John Flannigan had the jump on the Donnellys. For several weeks before the destruction of their barn, Flannigan had been rebuilding his own; it was half-completed, his horses were ready and his coaches in running order. He hired additional workers and went on building with added energy. The result was that the Donnellys had hardly secured the lumber for their own barn when Flannigan had finished his, and once more his coaches were rolling — the only stageline on the road. That was around October 15.

Nine nights later, on October 24, 1875, John Flannigan's barn was again reduced to ashes. Once more his coaches had been sawn apart and made useless, while his horses were so horribly mutilated they had to be destroyed!

CHAPTER ELEVEN

In the Reign of Terror

Poisoned cattle died in the fields,
Beneath those blazing skies;
While riders thundered down sideroads,
With wild, triumphant cries.

— Old Song

Someone, somewhere, at some time or other, somehow wrote something about, "In the spring a young man's fancy lightly turns to thoughts of love."

Shortly after old man time ushered in 1876, the house of Donnelly, although it was faced with thirteen different criminal charges — the boys had been working overtime — to be held at the Spring Assizes, charges of incendiarism, poisoning, brawling, wanton destruction and highway robbery, looked forward to a wedding and the eventual patter of little feet. Clubfooted William had fallen in love. The girl in the case — brave, crazy or both — was Nora Kennedy.

In later years William once thoughtfully declared: "I don't think my wife's folks ever cared a great deal about me."

Come to think of it, he might have had something there. After all, Nora Kennedy's mother had said, "I would rather see my daughter in her grave than married to a Donnelly," and turned her picture to the wall. Nora's father went one better; he threw the picture right out of the house, along with Nora, who had to seek the sanctuary of Donnelly walls till the hour of her wedding.

Nor can it be said that Nora's brother, John, manifested any love for his newly acquired in-laws. It was his tip-off that sent three constables, Bowden, Reid and Courcey, to break up William Donnelly's wedding party; later he was to be one of the six who went on trial, as being the ringleaders of the mob that massacred the Donnellys, and John Kennedy was one of the three accused of firing the shotguns that riddled John Donnelly to pieces. Slugs that were meant for William. Yes, there seems little cause to doubt William's words, "I don't think my wife's folks ever cared a great deal about me."

The wedding of Nora and William was typically Donnelly with all the trimmings — shouts, brawls, drunkenness, a run-in with the law and an attempted murder. Shuren a grand time was had by all!

It was on a cold February morning in 1876, with a slate sky overhead, when several cutters, icicles adorning the nostrils of the horses and sleigh bells jingling, pulled up before the church to announce the arrival of the Donnellys for the wedding ceremony. The same church was later the site for their funeral services. William had put a down payment on a house and acres, where he intended to take his bride; a small, one-story and four-roomed frame house, on the 9th Concession and three miles from the home of his parents. In later life he moved to Usborne Township.

Present for the wedding that day were old Jim and Johannah, their seven handsome sons, the bride-to-be — and no one else except the priest and a few church mice. The Donnelly charm, you know.

Driving into Lucan, the wedding party was held in the several rooms William had rented in Fitzhenry's Hotel. The party got off to a whale of a start. Crossing the lobby, Tom Donnelly spotted someone sitting there he didn't like. There was a slight pause while he mopped the floor with the man, before kicking him out into the street as Johannah applauded. Tom was the recognized fistic champion of the Donnellys, though each of them was a match for two ordinary men. After the delay in the lobby, the wedding party proceeded on to the banquet hall.

There, after a few snifters, Johannah, with tearfilled eyes, told the bride that weddings always made her sad, that she wanted Nora to call her "mother" and be as a sister to "my foin boys."

Around two that afternoon, the steady din of loud voices, the screeching of William's violin and the clatter of dancing feet, intermingled with the occasional Donnelly war-whoops and the bangs of falling chairs, as well as the steady output of bottles and glasses from the bar to the merrymakers, told those downstairs that the wedding party was still going strong.

Then three men whose stern features told they had not come to participate in the revelries, entered Fitzhenry's Hotel. The trio consisted of Constable Bowden and two deputies, Reid and Courcey. Word had just reached Bowden that James Jr. and John Donnelly had been seen riding away at the midnight hour, some six weeks earlier, from the burning barn of a farmer whose lips were sealed with terror.

The bride's own brother, John Kennedy, was the informer.

The trio, only Bowden was armed, broke in on the wedding party just as Johannah was in the middle of her rendition of "The Cat In The Corner." A lot of patience, a stroke of luck and several letters to Ireland, was finally able to place the words of the ditty, written at least a hundred and fifty years ago and probably more, in the hands of the writer.

"Oh weep for the day we were forced from our cot,
From our praties and milk and our stirabout pot;
When Judy kept every thing piping and hot,
So snug with the cat in the corner.

A scythe was stuck here, and a raping-hook there,
And Paddy's shillelagh, the pride of the fair,
Was placed in the chimney to sason with care,
Just over the cat in the corner.

Our windows so clane, by an unlucky stroke,
Had three of the purtiest panes in it broke.
We fastened up two with the tails of a coat,
And the smoke went through one in the corner.

Our dresser was dicked out in illegent style,
The trenchers an noggins your heart would beguile;
And the goose she was hatching her eggs all the while
Right by the cat in the corner.

Och! Paddy's the boy, with a stick in his fist,
With a spur in his head, and a bone in his wrist,
And a straw round his hat — you must call a gold twist,
Or he'll murder you all in the corner!"

It is still a mystery, as to all that was said and occured in those upstairs rooms. However, men who were in the lobby and bar of the hotel later told, that in less than five minutes from the time the officers ascended the stairs, there were loud shouts, the overturning of furniture and the sounds of a furious melee. Then Bowden, Reid and Courcey came rolling and bounding down the stairs like barrels, their clothes torn, their features battered and bleeding.

The bad boys of Biddulph followed right behind them, William in the lead and all of them tipsy.

Scrambling to his feet, Bowden turned to those who had come from the bar, attracted by the noise. "Help, men!" he began. "I'm calling on everyone of you to assist me and my deputies — ." He broke off when he suddenly realized he had no deputies. After gaining their feet they had kept right on going, and were on the roadway, ever widening the distance between them and the hotel. Bowden cast a hurried glance at the hardy lot descending the stairway, another to those legging it up the street; then yelling "Judas!" he promply forgot dignity and station, and followed the example of his deputies, "hightailing it hot and heavy."

Somehow William Donnelly had secured Bowden's revolver. He had had it in his hand when he descended the stairway, and making his way to the door he fired twice at the fleeing officer. In his alcoholic state he might have seen two Bowdens and fired at the wrong one. In any case, both shots went wild, one of them tearing into a tree near the roadway. Clubfooted Billy threw the gun with an exclamation of disgust and watched till the three in the roadway had vanished; then he and his brothers returned to the party, that continued on without interference till sundown.

But Bowden and his men, despite their inglorious retreat, had the last laugh. They had been worsted that day, but the following morning, re-inforced by deputies from surrounding villages, they went to William's newly purchased home and cut short his honeymoon — breaking into the house and surprising him as he sat down to eat breakfast.

After a furious struggle, during which he fought his way out of the house and into the front yard, William Donnelly was finally handcuffed, carried to a wagon and taken to the Lucan jail. The news of his capture spread. A group of angry farmers, with ideas of their own and a rope, stormed the jail that night, and were repulsed only after the gunfire of the constable forced them to retreat. Taken to trial for the shooting at Constable Bowden, William Donnelly was found guilty and sentenced to nine months imprisonment. Certainly a very light sentence. Still in handcuffs, cursing and struggling with his captors, he was led away.

That same night three masked men jumped Constable Bowden at a lonely spot and gave him the savage beating that permanently disabled him, forced him to resign his office and eventually cost him his eyesight. Bowden was unable to prove the identity of his attackers.

The spring of 1876 found the Donnellys faced with two big problems. One was to beat the thirteen criminal charges they had to face. The other was to keep the coachline going during William's imprisonment.

One Patrick James O'Shea, a farmer, had charged Mike Donnelly with assault and robbery, claiming Mike had beaten him up and taken his wallet, containing forty-three dollars, as well as his gold watch. O'Shea was loud in declaring that he was one man who wasn't afraid to appear in court against the Donnellys. On a night, about a week before the case came up for trial, three masked men rode up to the O'Shea farmhouse around midnight. They kicked in the door and dragged O'Shea from his bed into the kitchen, with the explanation, "We've something to show you."

O'Shea later said, despite the masks, that he recognized the three as Tom, John and Robert Donnelly. Two of the men holding his arms, the third — O'Shea said it was Tom — had several playing cards in his hand and was standing by the kitchen table. "Pull him over here, boys," Tom was quoted as saying, "I want to show him a trick — a damn good one!" On the bare wood of the kitchen table, Tom Donnelly then manipulated the cards till they were assembled into a small card-house. He turned to O'Shea.

"Now we'll just pretend this house of cards is your house," he announced. "It's erect and standing." From the several matches in his hand, he threw two inside the card-house, adding: 'And that's you and your wife inside it, snug and safe. But if you journey to court and press any charges, someone might come along and —.'

He lit another match and held its flame against the card-house till it burst into fire. "You see what can happen, don't you?" he went on to O'Shea. "And you're seeing just what will happen if you start talking out of turn. Give the matter some thought — when you wake up!" With that he lashed out his right hand in the vicious blow that crashed squarely into O'Shea's face, plunging him backwards to the floor. The three, after turning over chairs and cupboards, with broken dishes littering the floor, left the house. O'Shea's wife heard the hoofbeats of their horses fade into the night.

Patrick James O'Shea did not appear in court to press charges against Mike Donnelly.

Others scheduled to bring charges against the Donnellys at the Spring Assizes, received similar treatment and warnings of impending chaos, if they made any court appearance. Timothy Toohey, a farmer and local auction-eer, who did considerable traveling around the country and whose only sin against the house of Donnelly was his steady patronage of the Flannigan coachline, had suffered the loss of two poisoned cows and named the Donnellys as the poisoners. Masked riders paid him a night call, and warned of the folly of any court procedure. He was told, "Your friend, Flannigan, has had his barn burned down several times. How would you like to be tied, tossed into your own and have it come down over your head?"

Dennis O'Heenan, who had brought a charge against Tom Donnelly for stealing farm equipment, did not appear in court when the time came to press said charge. A visit from the night riders, that resulted in two blackened eyes and a broken arm, caused him to change his mind. Jere-miah Harrigan, who was to testify against the Donnellys was pulled from his cutter and given the vicious pommel-ing that made him decide to remain out of court.

Even the Quigley sisters, wishing to get into the swing of things, were preparing to appear against the Donnellys. It seemed, in the spring of 1876, that nearly everyone in Biddulph Township had some grievance against the Don-nellys that had to be settled in court.

The Quigley sisters, two spinsters in their fifties, lived in a small frame house just beyond Lucan's limits, where they wound up the clock, put out the cat and peeked under the bed with nightly diligence. Their story, and they intended to take it to court, named old Jim Donnelly as the fiend they had seen sneak around in back of their house one night and diabolically set fire to the old family — family — well, to a small but important building in rural life; one that was later made famous by Chic Sale.

But when the time for the Spring Assizes arrived, neither the Quigley sisters nor anyone else, with the sole exception of one Patrick Breen, appeared to press charges against the Donnellys. Breen, a stubborn man who had refused to be frightened into silence, claimed that his being a supporter and patron of the Flannigan coachline, as well as his participating in the Lucan battle as a Flannigan helper, had resulted in the poisoning of five of his cows. But he had not, or at least was unable to produce any conclusive proof that the poisoners were Biddulph's bad boys, and they were released.

The aftermath? It was not long in coming. The following day as he did his spring ploughing, a musket ball, fired from the brush at the far end of one field, whizzed scant inches past Patrick Breen's head. Two nights later another flew through his kitchen window and snapped the pipe from Breen's mouth as he sat before the stove. Before the month had passed, his house as well as his barn and out-houses, had gone up in flames!

With William in prison, things went from bad to worse for the Donnelly coachline. Brother James summed up the business one day with the words, "I'm getting damn sick of driving empty coaches up and down the road, with nothing to show for it but bird droppings!"

On the other hand, John Flannigan was being fairly deluged with business. When his barn had been fired for the second time, for awhile it seemed he had come to the end of the road; there were many who thought he would toss in the sponge. But John Flannigan could take it. Again telling he would fight fire with fire, Flannigan had erected another barn, secured new horses and equipment, and his coaches were rumbling along the roads once more.

Also, any would-be arsonists who came to his barn in the future, would be greeted with lead. Flannigan and his drivers made it a point to see that at least two of them — fully armed — were in the barn at all hours.

Flannigan's barn remained standing — this time — but he had a few bad minutes of his own during the summer of 1876. Driving the early morning run one day from Lucan to Exeter, a musket ball, fired from an adjoining field, tore into the side of his coach. "One of the Donnellys, of course," was Flannigan's explanation. "Only the Donnellys could be such poor shots. They should stick to their clubs and fists." A few weeks later, in an evening dusk and returning from London, Flannigan was again shot at by a figure that rose up behind a rail fence paralleling the road. Again the shot flew wide. John Flannigan grabbed his rifle, wheeled in his seat and fired into the gathering gloom.

A howl of pain and several oaths, heard by all the passengers, told he had scored a hit of some kind. But Flannigan didn't wait to investigate; he whipped up the horses and sent them galloping into Lucan. There the constable organized a small party, and accompanied by Flannigan, rode out to the scene of the shooting. They discovered a trail of crushed grass that led to the roadway, as well as a discarded bandana handkerchief, stained with blood. But at the road the trail was lost and the identity of the wounded man was never learned.

In September, continuous months of being in the red forced the Donnellys to give up the coachline. James sold out the business to a man named Collins, who was able, with the Donnellys out of the picture, to make a fairly good thing of it till the expanding rails of the iron horse antiquated all coachlines.

James had sold out in September of 1876. At that time William was still in jail, and his bride of one night dwelt alone in their small love nest with only memories. Along with old Jim and Johannah, the Donnelly homestead now sheltered only Tom, James and Robert, with the latter working part time in London. John and Patrick were working steadily in London and resided there. Foot-itchy Mike had hit the trail again and, after reaching Kingston, three hundred miles away, secured berth on a freighter that was dropping anchor at various ports of call on Lake Ontario.

It seems that around the Hamilton district, he had some run-in with the police that resulted in free flops and meals on the house for sixty days.

Mike was the only out and out shiftless member of the Donnellys. To give credit where it is due, for all their faults the rest were all good workers and not a lazy bone among them. But Michael seemingly preferred to drift around the countryside and follow blue horizons to honest toil. He would return frequently to the old homestead with tales of his travels but little else. He never fooled old Johannah. The story is told of the time when Mike, after several months of extensive travel, returning to the family with the usual empty belly and pockets, walked unexpectedly into the kitchen with the dramatic announcement, "Mother, I've come home to die," Johannah's truthful and brief reply was:

"You're a liar — you've come home to eat!"

James Donnelly Jr. robbed the Granton Post Office on a night in October, 1876. As a clever, leave-no clues thief, he would have made a first class garbage collector.

After forcing the rear door of the post office, around 11 p.m., and creating the din that awoke half the village, he lit the lantern he had brought along and allowed its beams to flood through the windows as beacons, while he began an unhurried search for swag. Two village night hawks, attracted by the light, saw and recognized James

Donnelly as he left the building. For some reason, dawn was well advanced when a constable and two deputies finally rode up to the Donnelly farmhouse, to learn that the wanted man had galloped away from there, less then twenty minutes earlier.

The posse took up a hot chase, stopped and questioned several travelers they met enroute, then finally sighted and overtook the fugitive on a sideroad about ten miles outside of London.

James Donnelly had been poorly mounted that morning. True, for the final few miles of the chase, his shouts, blows and kicks, kept the old nag he rode at the top of its speed, but that was no hell. At last, seeing the others were drawing ever nearer and knowing ultimate capture was inevitable, he pulled his horse to a stop, dismounted and awaited his pursuers. He still had one hope — a lone alternative. When his pursuers had reined-in and slid from their horses, they learned what it was; his hard fists and years of fistic training.

James Donnelly not only handled the trio as though they were paper men; when he rode on, leaving the three of them — yes, the three of them — groggy and on the ground behind him, he was riding the horse of one of them. Make no mistake about it. They may have known little or nothing about it. They may have known little or nothing about guns, but those Donnellys could handle their fists. Plenty!

Eventually reaching the Windsor border, James Jr. made his way to Detroit where he remained in hiding for the following seven months, returning home only in time to die.

Nothing of note occurred during the remainder of that fall, but in December William Donnelly, having completed his sentence, returned to the district and things started popping again. William fully blamed Constable Bowden for his incarceration, and after being sentenced had declared, "My only regret is that I missed the bastard when I shot at him!" Of course by the time clubfooted Billy was released, Bowden had long been gone from the district and his whereabouts unknown to Biddulph's bad boys, which was just as well for the ex-constable.

However, when William Donnelly returned he told he still had "other fish to fry," and a short while later the night skies of the Lucan district again started to flame the now familar orange hue. Within a period of less than seven weeks, five more barns were burned; in each case the owner was known to be at deadly enmity with the Donnellys.

There was a lull after the fifth fire, and the winter months dragged along. Then came March 17, 1877, and the usual reign of frolic and spirits — bottled — around Lucan, as the O'Brians, O'Maras, the Caseys, the Kelleys, McCarthys, Heenans, Sullivans and other families, gathered to honor their patron saint and recalls tall stories of the auld sod. But there were some that day in the area whose thoughts were not all jovial.

Around midnight, eight men met in the biting cold, at a lonely spot near Biddulph's Swamp Schoolhouse — the same structure where the township's vigilantes were later to organize and hold their secret meetings.

Made ruthless by ruthlessness, the eight had a final check-up on their plans, then mounted and rode till the object of their ride loomed before them — the Donnelly farmhouse.

By then it was around 1 a.m. and the house was in darkness. Leaving their horses they crept forward, fired the house, returned to their mounts and waited while flames swept higher through the blackness. The fire was well under way before voices sounded from within; the next moment the awakened Donnellys came hurrying through the front doorway and into the open. The horsemen started shooting, as had been planned. Five shots were fired in all before they galloped away, but the only casualty was the slight flesh wound, hardly more than a scratch, that Tom received in the shoulder.

But none of the Donnellys would ever dream of letting such a trifling thing as a bullet wound keep them from what promised to be a fight. Perish the thought.

While Johannah bolted out to the road and hurled curses after the retreating riders, Tom, along with Robert and old Jim, secured their clubs then hurried for their horses and gave chase. But they were unable to either overtake or learn the identity of their attackers, and finally lost them altogether in the darkness, after a three mile ride and near what is now Highway 4.

The following morning the news of the latest outrage swept over the district like wildfire. "The Black Donnellys — their house was burned down last night and they were shot at!" Eyes widened and jaws dropped at the words. For the first time, the foes of the Donnellys had attacked their stronghold — brought the war right into the camp of the enemy. Then dire prophecies began to be heard. All those who knew Jim and Johannah and the wild brood that was theirs, were well aware as to what the future would mean and shuddered at the thought of it.

And old Grandma Bell, the district's centenarian and noted fortune teller, who had been well on in years before Jim Donnelly came to Lucan, hit the nail on the head with the words: "Nights of hell are bound to follow!"

For sheer savagery, the retaliations of the Donnellys were appalling. What is more, they announced their intentions, well in advance. Then they did them.

The Donnelly farmhouse had been burned down shortly after 1 a.m. When the early stage from Lucan to London pulled out at seven o'clock that morning, Johannah,
her almost habitual scowl working overtime, and her
miniature Vandyke cruelly revealed in the sunlight, was
one of the passengers. When she returned that evening,
with a letter to Mike already in the mail, her sons John
and Patrick were with her. A fellow passenger in the
coach told that they made the journey in steely silence.
They got off the stage when it reached the Roman Line a
mile outside of Lucan, where old Jim awaited with wagon
and horses. They got in beside him, rumbling off into the
sunset and towards home. At least the charred embers they
now called home.

That same night five of the bad boys, William, Tom,
John, Robert and Patrick, along with their sire, rode hell-
for-leather into Lucan, up its main street then down and
around its side ones, with a series of high shrill shouts,
that struck terror into the hearts of housewives and caused
their lords uneasy moments. Finally the six pulled up
before the old Dominion Hotel and the score or so who
had stepped out onto the verandah, attracted by the noise
from the street. There old Jim, fist raised and trembling
with rage, cried out:

"We'll find who did it! One by one we'll get the men
who fired our house, if we have to ride up and down these
roads from now till Judgement Day! The rest of you are
going to be sorry you were ever born! Every damn one of
you will learn to fear us till you tremble in your boots!"
With that Jim Donnelly wheeled his horse, shouted to his
sons, "Come on, we've lots to do!" and galloped out of
Lucan, with Biddulph's bad boys behind him; while those
on the porch hurried to their homes to spend a sleepless
night, gun in hand, behind locked doors.

The Black Donnellys were going to ride again!

They did!

It wasn't long before galloping hooves were again being heard on the roads in and around Lucan, to announce the beginning of what was probably the most violent period in the entire thirty-three years feud, as night riders "hurried down sideroads with wild, triumphant cries," and the skies behind them once more blazed an angry red.

The Donnelly feud had always been a series of hostilities, lulls, more hostilities then more lulls; a sort of off-again, on-again affair. But the peak of its savagery appears to have been from around the end of March till the middle of May, 1877. And it was during that period, when, as at other times in the surrounding villages of Exeter, Granton and Centralia, the inhabitants, thankful they were out of the Lucan area, would point to the far-off, and almost nightly flame-lit skies, then exclaim the familiar: "The work of the Black Donnellys! Up to their old tricks again!"

In those villages, the writer has talked to no less than seven different persons, then youngsters, who clearly recall hearing the words and seeing those distant glows, as well as the final one that told of the massacre of the Donnellys.

There was an interval, however, between the time Jim Donnelly spoke his words before the hotel and the beginning of that deluge of destruction. First there was the matter of rebuilding the Donnelly farmhouse. It was early spring and the ground still hard: but with Johannah staying at William's place, and Jim and his five sons living in the barn on the farm, and near their work, a log house soon began to take form. When it was half finished, wandering Mike arrived, strolling in from somewhere, and now seven strong, in less than three weeks the new house was livable. Other partitions were later added at time periods, and just before its utter demolition the Donnelly farmhouse was one of the best in the district.

In this modern day, with the enforcement of the law invariably rigid and speedy to the transgressor, it may seem almost incredible to the reader, that a family could get away with all the depravities attributed to the Black Donnellys.

Frankly, after viewing those records of yesterday, in the light of today, it does seem hard to swallow. The Donnelly feud was more than a century ago, but even then there were those who could not believe such a state of affairs could exist. People living outside the Lucan area were unable to understand how such a reign of lawlessness and violence could manage to keep going, and for so long a period. A London reporter, equally bewildered, wrote the following interview with a prominent member of the Lucan community, only a few days after the Donnelly massacre, that appeared in the London Advertiser:

"Reporter: 'What do you think of the men that killed the Donnellys'?"

"Lucanite: 'Fine men. If it were known, it will be found that the murderers are the most respectful people in the township, good farmers and honest men. But they had to do it — there was no other way. People cannot live in a state of terror forever'."

"Reporter: 'Surely you could have done something about it. Was there no law'?"

"Lucanite: 'Law? Well I'll be damned! Law? What good was law around here? When did anybody ever get the best of the Donnellys in law? We never saw them up and get their desserts. They had everyone in the district scared out of their wits, and no one dared to appear against them'."

"Reporter: 'But how about the local authorities, the constable —'."

"Lucanite: 'Constable? Don't make me laugh! The Donnellys beat up every new constable as fast as we brought them in, as well as any other law enforcement. We have our own pride around here, we didn't want to take our tales of woe elsewhere and make others skin our skunks. The Donnellys were our problem, and we handled the matter in the only way possible. We wiped them off the face of the earth!' "

As soon as the Donnelly farmhouse had been completed, the fires began to break out again and terror was abroad.

The identity of the eight men that fired the Donnelly farmhouse has never been determined, but it is a safe bet that half the countyside knew. The retaliation of the bad boys of Biddulph, who were evidently working on the theory, strike out at all of them and you're bound to get the right ones. For a period that must have seemed endless to those in the Lucan area, the odds were two to one against any night traveler reaching his destination in safety. Farmers, homeward bound, would be pulled from cutters, buggies and wagons, and savagely beaten, sometimes tied to trees and horsewhipped by masked men, though the masks seemed hardly necessary.

However, the masks served one purpose. If some victim was brave or foolish enough to take the matter to court, he would be unable to positively identify his attackers.

As the writer of the old song put it, "The countryside became a place that lived in fear of night," for that was when danger was abroad. Housewives dreaded every sunset. Night after night saw masked vandals galloping over various sections of Biddulph, to burn, poison, mutilate and terrorize. An old issue of a Toronto newspaper, The Globe, informs that there were several cases of derailed trains, though just how their destruction would benefit the vandals, is hard to determine.

The barn of Jim Kelly went up in flames, while hoof-beats and shouts of triumph faded into the blackness. The house and barns of Michael Marra were utterly destroyed, then those of Dan McDonald. The farms of Ed Sullivan, Pat Dorsey, Jim Corrigan, Jim Toohey, Martin Ryan and Bill Casey, along with others, knew the presence of the arsonists. The herds of Tom Kinsella, John Cain, and both John and William Thompson, were found poisoned. The mutilated horses of Jim Barnes and Martin Darcey had to be destroyed. Then there was the Lamphier fire, the Dewan fire, the Bruin fire, the Hodges fire, the Harrigan fire, the Blake fire, the Kehoe fire —.

And on and on rode those masked riders, into and through the village of Lucan, down highways and lonely sideroads with their wild shouts rising to the stars; past broad fields and isolated farmhouses, where families, whitefaced behind locked doors, heard the approach of those dreaded shouts and hoofbeats and prayed they would go by, while husbands whispered "It's them!" and mothers silenced frightened children to awed stillness with that terrible threat: "Hush or the Black Donnellys will get you!"

Then around the middle of May came a sudden lull in hostilities — and death!

In a sunset, on the evening of May 12, 1877, a passenger on the Lucan-bound stage, a wan featured man who carried a small satchel and coughed frequently, asked the driver to let him off at the Roman Line, a mile outside the village. It was James Donnelly Jr., the grim reaper near, returning to his people.

The driver of the Flannigan stage that evening, a comparative newcomer to the district, had failed to recognize James Donnelly; but eventually news of his return got around and reached the ears of the law. Two nights later several constables rode up to the farmhouse, but it was evident and an attending doctor affirmed the fact, that James Donnelly's hours on this earth were rapidly coming to a close. An unsuspected heart ailment, along with the cold that had developed into pneumonia, brought death to him around 4 a.m. the following morning, May 15, 1877.

His last words were whispered to Johannah, who hovered above his bed while his father and brothers stood near. "Don't let me fall to sleep, Mother. I'm afraid of the dark!"

CHAPTER TWELVE

The Man Who Didn't Fear the Donnellys

Then came one day to Lucan Town,
A man of mighty frame.
His beard was black, his shoulders broad;
James Carroll was his name.

— Old Song

"Weapons of the weak — fit only for cowards!"

That was old Jim Donnelly's opinion of firearms. He never used them himself, and generally regarded anyone who did as being about ninety-nine and seven-eighths percent yellow. Johannah shared his views. Like his sons, old Jim was strictly a fists and club man.

On the whole, guns played a very small part in the Donnelly feud, making it unique, perhaps, for that very reason. This can be understood, of course, when one remembers that nearly all of its participants, coming from the land of the shamrock, lived in the days when a strong fist and a stout club were practically regarded as the national weapons. True, William Donnelly was jailed for shooting at Constable Bowden. Later, Robert was to take pot-shots at the law — likewise without success. There is no recorded incident of a Donnelly bullet ever hitting its target, however. Terrors though they were

123

with their fists and clubs, anything they shot at was perfectly safe.

Following the death of James Donnelly Jr., in May 1877, there was another lull in hostilities. Patrick and John returned to their jobs in London. Roving Mike hit the road again, and for awhile graced the cities of Toronto and Hamilton with his presence. That left only Robert and Tom on the farm with old Jim and Johannah, as William lived with his wife on their own place, three miles away.

It was around December 1877, when the barn of a farmer named Blake was burned one night. There does not appear to be any sound reason as to why it should have been the work of the Donnellys, as it was later brought out that they hardly knew him and had nothing to gain by destroying his property. But Robert and William were named as the arsonists and Lucan's newest constable, a recent arrival named Everett, rode out and put them through the third degree, with charges both men hotly denied. As nothing could be proved, the charges were eventually dropped.

A short while later Everett was given a bad beating, just outside of Lucan, by two masked men he "thought could have been William and Robert Donnelly."

Then came a night in March 1878, with Constable Everett entering the rear door of the house he occupied, when he was fired at, three times, by Robert Donnelly who, filled with the juice of joy, shot from behind a nearby woodpile. Of course all the shots flew wide, as was inevitable when fired by a Donnelly, but Everett's answering fire had a certain amount of accuracy. One of his two bullets plunged through Robert Donnelly's shoulder, spinning him to the ground, probably more drunk than hurt. The constable, gun in readiness, then handcuffed and ensconced him in the local jug.

Awakening from his jag in the morning and seeing the barred windows, his first words to his jailor were, "Where am I?"

Robert Donnelly was tried and sentenced to two years imprisonment. Johannah, loudly bewailing the verdict and little knowing she would never see her son again, bade him a tearful farewell and departed from the courtroom with the lament, "My poor boy missed that constable because he was drunk at the time of the shooting. God's curse on the whisky!"

After the Everett shooting, there was another interval of comparative peace in the Lucan district. Then in the early winter of 1879, there came the news that must have struck the Donnelly family as a bolt from the blue. Brother Mike went to work! He not only secured employment in a wagon factory in London, he actually held the job for almost seven months! It proved that the days of miracles were not over.

Time marched on a bit, with spring bringing nothing more than several petty quarrels between the Donnellys and their neighbors. But the summer of that year, 1879, brought about the destruction of McRobert's Old Dominion Hotel and Fitzhenry's Hotel, as well as the beginning of what was to be the end for the Donnellys.

On a Saturday night in June, William and Tom Donnelly rode into Lucan and entered the bar of Fitzhenry's Hotel, the same house where William had held his memorable wedding party. As usual the place was filled with the farmers who had driven into the village from surrounding districts, to while away a few sociable hours as their wives did the Saturday night's shopping and gossiped with neighboring farm wives. And as usual, drinking by themselves, William and Tom received only silence and the hostile glares of the bar's inmates. But that never bothered them. The brothers downed several drinks, then William asked Fitzhenry, who was behind the bar with two helpers:

"Fitzhenry, I'm here to help you. You'd like your hotel to be able to serve the best meat in the district wouldn't you? Well, you'll be able to do just that, if you start buying it from us."

Both Fitzhenry's answer and eyes were cold. "I have a man who supplies me with meat."

"We know you have, and we know who it is," put in Tom Donnelly.

"And we can undersell him," informed William. "Well, how about it, Fitzhenry?"

The others in the bar had ceased talking and were attentive listeners. They were at least thirty strong, and all of them hated the Donnellys. Fitzhenry knew it, and realized they would be for him in the event of trouble. It may have prompted him to answer William Donnelly with a laugh, then ask: "Suppose I do buy meat from you? Just who are you going to steal it from, to sell it to me?"

The listeners broke into loud guffaws at the reply. None of them had ever expected to hear anyone talk like that to a Donnelly. Neither had the two brothers. For an instant they stared at the proprietor as though unable to believe their ears. Then howling an oath, Tom Donnelly made as though to leap over the bar and grab Fitzhenry by the throat. But William, always quick with the gray matter, realized the hopelessness of the situation; that there were at least thirty of their enemies, all of them brawny and capable, waiting for a chance to fling themselves on him and his brother.

He grabbed Tom, held him back and whispered something in his ear. Then the two, arm in arm, made their way from the bar. In the doorway, William Donnelly turned and called out to the proprietor. "That was a good joke, Fitzhenry. Yes, sir, a good joke and right to the point. Which reminds me, we'll have to play one on you sometime."

Less then ten nights later, something was played on Fitzhenry, though if it was intended for a joke, its perpetrators had a weird sense of humor. Shortly before 2 a.m., on July 5, the night constable, Alfred Brown, from a distance saw three men run from the rear of Fitzhenry's Hotel, leap on their waiting horses and gallop off. Hurrying to investigate, Brown found the back end of the hotel in flames. He gave the alarm that aroused its inmates, but despite all efforts the fire soon spread through the old frame building, and though no lives were lost, Fitzhenry's Hotel was utterly destroyed.

Charlie McRoberts, who ran the Old Dominion Hotel, had long denounced the Donnellys, and had offered free drinks for a year to any man in the community who could whip Tom Donnelly. After seven years, the offer still stood.

The morning after the Fitzhenry fire, it was McRoberts who first suggested that the community form a vigilance committee. More than that, he offered the back rooms of his hotel for a meeting place. "The law wasn't able to prove who burned down Mike Madill's Hotel fourteen years ago, and we know it was the Donnellys!" declared McRoberts. "The law wasn't able to prove who burned down Fitzhenry's Hotel and we know it was the Donnellys. Alright, from now on we'll take matters into our own hands."

The news of the impending first meeting of a vigilance committee spread like wildfire, and met with the approval of the surrounding countryside. Now folks could unite, would be able to do things their own way and get rid of those Black Donnellys. Hurrah for Charlie McRoberts! Then came the word that the first meeting of the vigilance committee, "one of importance to every law-abiding person," would be held at the Old Dominion Hotel on the night of August 1. It was expected that everyone, with the exception of babes under five months and great-grandmothers over ninety-five, would attend.

But no one attended that meeting, for it was never held.

In the Stygian blackness just before the dawn of August 1, the Old Dominion Hotel was set aflame and burned to the ground. The arsonists? No one could prove who they were, but everyone seemed to know. And once again housewives living far out on the Roman Line, told of being awakened from their sleep and sitting up in bed, to harsh shouts of triumph and a mad clatter of hooves, hurrying by and towards the Donnelly place in the wee small hours before the dawn!

"Then came one day to Lucan Town a man of mighty frame."

James Carroll came from the village of Exeter, fourteen miles to the north of Lucan. A description of Carroll, when on trial for leading the massacre of the Donnellys, and written by a reporter of the day who was present at the trial, is a bit long-winded but paints a clear picture of "the man who didn't fear the Black Donnellys." The description reads:

"James Carroll stands six feet high and is stoutly built, being particularly heavy about the chest and shoulders. His head appears to be over the average size, and his neck exceptionally short and heavy. His head is covered with a thick growth of straight black hair, and he wears a very heavy mustache and Imperial, the former growing down past the corners of his mouth to the lower edge of the under jaw. His complexion is dark and sallow, and this with the peculiar cut of his beard, his small, dark and restless eyes, and his low and somewhat receding forehead constantly covered with long traverse wrinkles that extend almost from temple to temple, give him a somewhat sinister appearance. Some other features, however, in some measure counteract the general effect of these just named and perhaps the most striking of the redeeming features is that his eyebrows are finely arched."

Twenty-eight years of age and two hundred pounds of brawn, a former farmer, later a lumberjack and recently a dealer in farming equipment, James Carroll arrived in Lucan only a few days after the burning of the Old Dominion Hotel. By then Constable Everett, having received another beating at Donnelly hands, had gone the way of all former Lucan constables and resigned. The then present law enforcers — two of them — were somehow always out of sight when the Donnellys were around.

While James Carroll had what it takes, he was no modest violet when it came to admitting it.

In the Western Bar, his arrogant manner and loud boasts of personal valor, soon attracted the attention of the villagers. Throughout a long afternoon and downing enough giggle water to put an ordinary man under the table, he told one and all what a terror he was; that he'd like nothing better than a chance to spit in the devil's face and could lick his weight in wildcats. Around sundown, an awed assembly looking on, Carroll announced: "I've heard of the trouble you have had for years with the Black Donnellys, and you're looking at the man who can end it for you. That's why I'm here. Make me a special constable and I'll drive them to hell out of here in no time!"

Would they! They would — and how! Before old Sol had set, a petition for a special constable had been written up, that soon had a hundred and six signatures attached to it and was on its way to the judge of Middlesex County. The document, long considered one of the most unique in Canadian annals, read:

To William Elliot, Est., Judge of the County of Middlesex.

The humble prayer and petition of the undersigned inhabitants of the Township of Biddulph showeth as follows:

Whereas, for some time past evil-minded persons in the Township of Biddulph have been violating the laws and acting in such a manner as to endanger the persons and property of the peaceable portion of the inhabitants thereof and:

Whereas, from there being but a few constables in said Township, it is difficult and often impossible to have warrants or other processes of the Local Justices of the Peace executed; and in consequence thereof compelling injured persons to either refrain from taking legal proceedings for the redress of wrongs or go to the expense of laying complaints before the Justices of the Peace in the City of London; and:

Whereas, your petitioners are of the opinion that much of the above recited inconvenience would be obviated by the appointment of James Carroll, now of said township, as a Special Constable therein:

Your petitioners therefore pray that the said James Carroll be appointed as a Special Constable in and for this County, and your petitioners will ever pray."

And so James Carroll became a Lucan constable. His address in taking office consisted of fourteen words: "I will drive the Donnellys out of Lucan, if it costs me my life!"

CHAPTER THIRTEEN

Blood on the Moon

One hundred years old Grandma Bell,
Warned all and she would say:
'The sun is sinking and that means,
Danger is on the way.'
— Old Song

It took Charlie McRoberts' suggestion that a vigilance committee be formed to start the men of the Lucan territory to serious thinking, as to a way of ridding themselves of the menace that had so long plagued their countryside. But at least it was a step forward. It took James Carroll and his request that he be made a constable to combat the situation, to show there was now at least one man among them who was not afraid of Biddulph's bad boys. Another step.

However, it was the seemingly trivial incident of Thompson's lost cow that plainly revealed the handwriting was on the wall for the Black Donnellys.

Remembering his promise to get things done, once the newcomer, James Carroll, had been made constable, the countryside sat back to await developments. Following the burning of the old Dominion Hotel, there was another lull in activities drastic, but tension was in the air, a tension

that was ever mounting; the feeling that something powerful was soon to pop. Presently there were those in the
village who were telling that Constable Carroll, grim-faced
and secretive, was doing a lot of night riding; there were
mysterious little whisperings of "The Swamp Schoolhouse!"

August passed, then came September 1879, and the
case of the lost cow.

Living near Lucan was a farmer named Thompson, the
same Thompson whose destroyed harness shop was
rumored to have been burned by the Donnellys. One day
in September, a cow belonging to farmer Thompson up
and disappeared. Certainly there did not seem to be anything momentous about the matter, but before twelve hours
had passed, an observer would have thought the Crown
Jewels had been purloined. His herd at pasture, Thompson
first noticed the cow was missing at the morning milking,
then drove into Lucan to report the matter. Somehow the
news spread like wildfire; by noon everyone in the district
knew of it and once more the so familiar words were being
heard:

"The work of the Black Donnellys! Up to their old
tricks again!"

Fear can be driven just so far. Even the cowardly
jackal, if its fear is great enough, will turn and fight, and
when it does so it fights viciously — insanely. And the
inhabitants of Biddulph, fed up with years of fear and no
retaliation, had finally reached the point where they would
not only turn and fight — they would charge the enemy.
Somehow the incident of Thompson's lost cow seemed to
be the straw that broke the camel's back.

That afternoon the fields of many a Biddulph farm
were deserted. Men drifted into Lucan and gathered at
bars; there were angry voices and threats. Shortly after 2

p.m. a mob of forty, armed with clubs, were advancing on the Donnelly farmhouse!

Early that morning, before Thompson had ridden into the village to report his loss, James Carroll had journeyed to Exeter on official business, so knew nothing of the missing cow or the mob that had gathered and was advancing on the Donnelly farm.

Another, equally ignorant of the mounting crisis, was Tom Donnelly. The same morning Tom had caught the early stage for a few days visit with his three brothers, John, Mike and Patrick, who were working in London. The result made it a bad moment for old Jim and Johannah to be attacked by their enemies. With James Jr. dead, Robert in jail, William living three miles away, three of the boys in London and another on the way to visit them, the old couple, as fate would have it, were alone on the farm that day, probably for the first time in years.

By then, it should be remembered, old Jim was long past his fighting days, being in his sixty-third year and a victim of rheumatism for some time.

There was little or no planned strategy, the mob members even disdaining to wear masks. Reaching the farmhouse, unnoticed by its inmates, half of the men approached the front door; the rest, with John Flannigan among them, went around to the rear. The two Donnellys were in the kitchen at the time, Johannah with sleeves rolled up and kneading bread dough while her husband sat nearby, patching a length of binder canvas. There was no warning. The first inkling either of them had that danger was less than a thousand miles away, was when the door was suddenly kicked back with a bang and John Flannigan, along with several others and all of them carrying clubs — weapons symbolic of Erin's sons — were framed in the doorway. Behind them the two Donnellys could see more faces.

Exclaiming, "What the devil!" old Jim leaped to his feet.

"Stay where you are, Donnelly!" ordered Flannigan. "Try any of your tricks on us and you'll get a broken head!" One of the others shouted to Johannah: "That goes for you, too, you old she-devil!"

The front door burst open and hostile men poured through the opening, foremost among them being John Kennedy, the brother-in-law of William Donnelly. Jim and Johannah, denying that they knew anything of Thompson's missing cow, were placed in the centre of the kitchen and forced to stand there with raised hands, under the threat of menacing clubs. They were told: "Try doing anything, now, and hell will have two star boarders for supper!"

With the two Donnellys captured and helpless, some of the mob hurried to the barn to search for the missing cow; others made their way to the woods at the rear of the farm, thinking that the animal might be tethered there, till the search for it blew over. Finally, when they had all returned to the house, they admitted their quest had failed. Thompson's cow was not on the Donnelly farm.

"I tell you we know nothing of any stolen cow!" Johannah shrieked again and again. Jim Donnelly challenged every man in the mob, "if you snivelling skunks will come at me one at a time." When jeers greeted the challenge he cursed everyone of them, together then individually. Of course he knew them all and had for years.

It was a situation unique to every member of the mob. Here, after years of little more than wishful thinking, they had two of the hated Donnellys before them, helpless — utterly at their mercy. A spirit of vandalism crept over the gloating men. This was really something; a day of days.

Then as Jim Donnelly continued to shout at them, ordering them to leave the house, one member of the mob walked to a kitchen chair, picked it up and sent it flying through a window.

It was the awaited signal, all that the others needed; the next moment the mob proceeded to wreck the house.

Curtains were yanked from windows, pictures from walls, amid shouts of approval. A cabinet containing Johannah's best china, some of it brought from her home in the distant Galty Mountains, was sent crashing to the floor. Kitchen shelves and dishes were broken, preserves and dried fruits trampled into the floor. Handhewn and store-bought furniture was splintered. Beds in the bedrooms were overturned and broken; not one windowpane in the house escaped destruction. The hatred of years manifested itself.

While all this was going on, Jim and Johannah, trembling with rage, were helpless spectators, held fast in strong hands.

The mob left without any personal violence to the old couple, but there were many threats; threats that told them this was only the beginning, and that "both of you and those unhung devils you've raised had better get to hell out of the country while you're still alive! We won't be so gentle the next time!"

Once the mob had left, Johannah Donnelly did not pause to lament or take inventory of her losses. There was a vital matter of moment. While she and her husband had been held prisoners, the men around them had let drop enough chatter for her to know they intended to continue their search for the lost cow, and planned to march on the home of her son, William, three miles away. William had to be warned. But how? To go by horseback or buggy to his house would mean having to travel the same road her enemies were traversing, and they would be sure to stop her. Perhaps none too gently.

There seemed to be only one other way. True, she was almost fifty-six at the time, had put on weight in recent years and the plan she had would mean climbing fences, wading through two swift-moving creeks and running across open fields for long stretches at a time to reach the house of William before the mob arrived there. But one of her boys was in danger. It was enough for Johannah. Red flannels and all, she set off on her cross-country journey at a rapid pace, to warn the club-footed gentleman who fiddled while Biddulph burned.

Johannah almost ran into grief at the start. Pat Whelan, a neighboring farmer, saw her climbing his roadway fence, recognized her and charged forward — with a shotgun. "You couldn't blame me. I didn't know what hellery she was up to — maybe to poison some of my cattle!"

The gun didn't faze Johannah. Whelan heard a brief but scorching blast of adjectives, some of them suggesting he had canine ancestory, as she hurried past and on to far-away places. A short while later Johannah was chased by a grazing bull in one of the fields of an adjoining farm, and told how "I had to hustle my old behind," till she put a fence between her and the monster. Finally, exhausted, she reached the home of her son and told her tale to clubfooted Billy, who then went out on the porch to meet the enemy — a club in one hand, a gun in the other.

There he must have recalled something about, "Music hath charms to soothe the savage beast." He called for his wife to fetch him his bow and fiddle, and announced he would play for his visitors. While awaiting their arrival, he entertained Johannah and his wife with several renditions of jigs and reels.

Meanwhile, less than half a mile from the old Donnelly place, the mob started to break up. The big excitement over, enthusiasm began to wane; most of the men wanted to return to Lucan and tell of their recent triumph. Only John Kennedy and John Flannigan, along with four others, remained loyal to the cause. When the others left, the six continued on and finally reached the house of William Donnelly, to find its lord awaiting them on the porch, with gun in hand. His wife and Johannah were beside him.

William greeted his uninvited visitors with a mocking laugh and a sweeping bow of mock politeness. He called out a loud, "Good afternoon, gentlemen," sent his gaze to John Kennedy and added, "And you, too, dear brother-in-law," before cocking both barrels of his shotgun and inviting "Step forward and sample some Donnelly hospitality!"

The six men, coming to a sharp halt just outside the gate, declined the invitation.

William Donnelly then proceeded to challenge and insult all of them. He'd fight them if they came through the gateway one at a time; he'd let his mother hold the gun with the understanding she was to shoot the first one who came forward, other than his antagonist. When he had finished with one he would take on another; he promised to accommodate all six of them with speed and efficiency. Well, that was his offer. Any last questions? No? Then why the delay? Come, come, gentlemen — who will be first?

There were no takers. Jack Quinn, one of the six and a habitual bar fly, spoke up: "We came here to find Thompson's cow."

William Donnelly answered with, "I thought you might have come here to find your mother, Quinn." That retort must have hurt. It was well known that drunken and shiftless Jack Quinn had left his mother in a poorhouse in

Ireland. According to the testimony of John Kennedy, later given in court, "William Donnelly then laid down his gun, laughed at us, picked up his fiddle and started playing 'Bony Crossed The Alps'."

The six men standing beyond the gateway exchanged glances and finally decided they had done enough for one day; let someone else search for Thompson's cow. They had little stomach to face the fiddling gentleman on the porch, who beat out time with his clubfoot. His gun and club were too nearby. Besides — well, it had a been a long walk, the roads dusty, it was a hot day and their throats were dry. Again, Larkin's Inn, famed for its schooners of cold stout, with high collars and plenty of bang, was just a bit more than a mile up the road.

After a brief conference, the men were making tracks for the inn, hearing the scorn of the two women on the porch and the wailings from the battered fiddle of William, as he sawed out repetition after repetition of "Bony Crossed The Alps!"

History repeated itself the following morning.

Of course by then, everyone in and around Lucan for miles knew of the raid on the Donnelly farmhouse the previous day. There was rejoicing, with every member of the mob being lauded on highways and backroads. "Heroes, who have frightened the Donnellys," was the general opinion. But when the Collins' coach made the 7 a.m. run to London, the next morning, it was flagged to a halt at the Roman Line, a mile outside of Lucan and Johannah Donnelly got aboard.

Collin who was driving and had originally bought the coachline from James Donnelly turned to the one who sat beside him on the driver's seat. "The old woman herself!" he whispered. "Sure as God made little apples she's going to London to bring back her boys, just like the last time! There will be hell to pay!"

Words of truth.

Arriving in London, the determined Johannah first made tracks for the wagon factory that employed Mike Donnelly. Needless to say, it did not take any coaxing for him to throw up his job. Then she found the others. By noon Johannah had told everything to Mike, Pat, Tom and John, and the four, eyes flashing and vowing vengeance, were ready to return with her to the farm — this time to stay.

And it was that very afternoon, while awaiting the departure of the Lucan coach, when a little known happening occurred. Not feeling up to snuff, perhaps as a result of her three miles run on the previous day, Johannah, accompanied by her four handsome and stalwart sons, spied a doctor's sign and dropped into his office on London's Dundas Street. The doctor, tall, cross-eyed and newly-arrived in London, mixed her up an elixir then set the price at one dollar.

Johannah gasped. "What? A dollar? A — a whole dollar! Why — why you thieving blackguard!" She turned to her sons. "Pay this cross-eyed thief, Tom!"

Tom did, with the backhand swipe of his hand that sent the doctor to the floor with a bang. Then the five trooped out, leaving him sitting there with an open mouth and a sore behind, in the centre of his office.

Now that is all there is to the story itself, so trivial it would not have been set down here were it not for the identity of the doctor. A short while later he was to leave London, suspected of having poisoned a chambermaid. Going to Chicago, there accused of two more cases of poisoning, he was sent to the Illinois State Penitentiary at Joliet in November 1881. Released ten years later he journeyed to England, began a one-man war on prostitutes, eventually poisoned seven of them and became the most notorious murderer of the nineteenth century. He was hanged at London's Newgate prison, November 15, 1892. His name was Dr. Thomas Neill Cream.

Johannah, along with Mike, Tom, John and Pat, returned from London on the evening stage.

Collins, who was driving, saw them get off at the Roman Line, where old Jim was waiting with a wagon and horses. Once again they drove off into the sunset and towards the farmhouse, while Collins hurried the coach into Lucan to spread the alarm: "The boys are back! The old woman brought them back!" Of course Robert was still in jail, but with William, old Jim and Johannah, the Donnellys were now seven strong. Yes, Biddulph's bad boys were back.

And the fires began to break out again!

William Casey had been one of the men that raided the Donnelly farmhouse. He was the first to get it in the new resumption of hostilities.

Around midnight, on the same day the sons of Johannah Donnelly returned to the fold, galloping hooves were again heard far out on the Roman Line. Then five masked men rode up to the Casey farm. William Casey was dragged from his bed to the yard, tied to a tree and horsewhipped fiendishly. His horses were hamstrung, a torch applied to his barn and outhouses before the riders rode off, with loud shouts.

Once more terror gripped Biddulph, while swirling flames again stabbed up into the blackness of its night skies.

Then came other atrocities. The farms of Jim Corrigan, Jim Shea, Pat Breen, Pat Sweeney and at least four other men, all of whom had been in the raid on the Donnelly house, were visited by the night riders, who always left destruction and rising flames behind them when they rode away. Again the herds of Tom Kinsella and John Thompson were found poisoned: John Kennedy found blood-splashed stalls and mutilated horses in his barn. Pat Whelan, who had threatened Johannah with a shotgun, was attacked by three masked men, and while being given a fearful beating was told to, "Mind your manners the next time you talk to a lady, you bastard!" before he was pommelled into unconsciousness.

Why even the bull that chased Johannah was found with a leaden slug in its brain. By God, a Donnelly bullet had finally hit something!

Then around ten o'clock on a night in the following month — October — just as John Flannigan was leaving his barn, he had four visitors. His coaches put up, his horses bedded down for the night, Flannigan and a companion, one of his drivers, were ready to take their departure, when Tom, William, John and Mike Donnelly walked into his barn, "Just thought we would pay you a little visit, Flannigan," greeted Tom. "Returning that visit you made to our place."

The four brothers exchanged knowing smiles.

Flannigan instantly knew that night visit augured him no good, but he was a Tarzan in strength and utterly fearless. "Out to raise some more hell, eh?" he answered. "I've heard you're doing quite a bit of it lately."

William Donnelly turned to Tom, "Let me handle this," he said then addressed Flannigan. "Now is that a nice way to talk to visitors?" He went on: "You see, Flannigan, we've decided it's high time you should have hell beaten out of you. Now while any of the four of us are capable of doing the job, we talked it over to see who should have the honor."

Flannigan nodded: he understood. He asked, "Which one is it to be?"

"Tom, here," informed William. "Oh, he's a great one for keeping people in their place and making them stay there. Once he is through with you, Flannigan, you'll think twice after this before barging into houses where you are not wanted." William's chuckle revealed his teeth. "Again, in fighting him, there is a prize for you if you win," he reminded. "Years ago Charlie McRoberts offered free drinks for a year to any man who could lick Tom. No one has been able to do it yet, so now is your chance to earn yourself a year's supply of rye juice."

The barn was large and roomy; an ideal place for a rough-and-tumble. As Flannigan peeled off his coat, William turned to the driver. "Up against the wall, you, and no interference," he ordered. "We won't give any help, so don't you try to." Then, with both men in the center of the barn and ready, William called out:

"Go get 'em, Tom, and remember how he sassed mother." Tom leaped forward to the attack.

It was sheer murder. Flannigan's strength and horse-shoe bending was well known; again, he was forty pounds heavier than Tom. But it was sheer murder; Flannigan never had a chance. By all accounts told of him, Tom had a bobbing, weaving style when he fought, like that of Dempsey; and the Donnelly-Flannigan fight must have been similar to round one of the affair at Toledo, years later, when the Manassa Mauler literally annihilated the ponderous Jess Willard. Flannigan was up, then down; up again, down again, up again then down again. On his fifth trip to the earthen floor of the barn, all of them in a matter of less than three minutes, Flannigan, bleeding profusely, eyes closing and jaw broken, was unable to arise.

Tom then proceeded to administer the Donnelly coup de grace — the boots. Flannigan, helpless, was kicked repeatedly and viciously in the face, disfiguring him beyond all recognition, till he blacked out.

Not till then did William call Tom off and turn to the driver, a wide-eyed, speechless witness. "Remember you, he was beaten fairly and none of us interfered," William reminded. "When he comes to himself, tell him if he wants to take the matter to court, there is also that business of him leading the mob on our house. And remind him we can always pay him another visit. You understand?" The driver nodded.

The four Donnellys walked from the barn into the starlight and disappeared.

Old Jim and Johannah, unable to forget the raid on their farmhouse, brought action against most of the members of the mob, charging house-breaking, wanton destruction and trespass. But with their reputation, and having to break down the evidence of around forty respected citizens, they got nowhere and the case was thrown out of court.

However, vengeance could be extracted in another way, and hoofbeats and shouts continued to be heard along the Roman Line almost nightly, while flames mounted skyward.

It was on a night late in November 1879, with their vandalism in full swing, when old Jim Donnelly, along with Tom, John and Mike, pulled up their horses before the small log house of "Grandma" Bell, the district's noted centenarian and teacup reader, and the last of a black colony that had settled on the London and Goderich Road sixty years earlier. The old woman, who later told and retold the story to any who would listen, related it to a reporter:

"There was blood on the moon that night, and I was sitting right here in the kitchen. It was around nine o'clock when I heard their horses being pulled up before the house. The next moment they came through the door, the four of them, crazy drunk and laughing. I knew Mr. Donnelly and had spoken to him several times in the past. I had seen the others, too, and I knew they were his sons, but I didn't know which was which. Mr. Donnelly said: 'Granny, we want you to tell us our fortunes'.

"Then he pointed to one of his sons and said, 'This is Mike.' Mike smiled, waved his hat and shouted, 'Hello, Granny, I hope my fortune says I'm going to find five barrels of gold!'. The father pointed to another son and said, 'This is John'. John was a handsome man, though not as heavy as the others. He smiled and said 'Hello.' The father said 'And the other one is Tom'.

"I looked twice at Tom. I had heard he was the terrible man had beat so many men with his big fists. He did not smile, he didn't speak; he just stared at me and his eyes were cold.

"I knew they would not harm me. Mr. Donnelly had always been friendly and smiled when he saw me. Yet I did not want to tell them their fortunes, but when he asked me again I made some tea, and after they drank it I saw what was before them in the tea leaves. There was blood on the moon that night and I could see it all plainly.

"Mr. Donnelly asked, 'Well, Granny, what do you see?' And I told him, 'I see death, Mr. Donnelly; death for you, death for your wife and your sons here! I see death for all of you — soon and terrible!'

"They laughed at me; oh, how they shouted and laughed. Mr. Donnelly threw a coin on the table, and said my words were the funniest he had ever heard. Then they all ran out and got on their horses. I could still hear them laughing as they rode up the road. The next I heard of them was when a neighbor ran over to tell me they were all dead! They — Mrs. Donnelly, Mr. Donnelly, John, Tom and Mike — had all been murdered!"

CHAPTER   FOURTEEN

The Gathering of the Vigilantes

Came that cold winter's night,
With James Carroll at their head,
When the mob broke into Donnelly's house,
To find Donnelly in bed.

— Old Song

"Never fear, mother, I'll be back home in plenty of time to help you eat the Christmas goose." Those were the last words Mike Donnelly was destined to ever speak to Johannah. The next time she saw him he was in his coffin.

Shortly after John Flannigan received his savage beating at the hands of Tom Donnelly, in October, there came another lull in hostilities. Then around December of the same year, 1879, and with all temporarily peaceful and quiet, foot-itchy Mike got that urge to hit the broad highways for a spell; one that could not be quenched despite the cold winds and snow of winter. Mike had saved some money during his recent months of employment, and in former travels had made the acquaintance of one who had become a bosom crony.

The friend lived near Port Dover, around eighty miles to the north. Mike spoke about traveling up that way and spending a few days with him before Christmas. But for some reason his visit exceeded the intended period. Christmas Eve found Mike Donnelly, in the company of two other knights of the road, in an abandoned shed near New Waterford Station, and still seventy miles from home.

The three were gathered around the fire they had started on the earthen floor, while winter winds whistled without; but Mike Donnelly's hopes of spending Christmas day with the family were still high. He knew that a freight train, due to pass along around midnight, would stop while the engine took on water. It would get him into London before dawn; he could catch the early Lucan-bound coach and be at the farmhouse by noon — in time to help eat the Christmas goose.

Mike still had a few dollars on him — fourteen to be exact — as well as the small satchel he carried. Being Christmas Eve, the three were making merry around a whiskey jug while awaiting the oncoming freight.

It was around 11 p.m. and bitterly cold when the firewood ran out. Mike volunteered to go to a nearby woodpile, but on his return found that two wandering and unemployed lumberjacks — burly, bewhiskered and surly brutes — had been attracted by the light from the fire, entered the shed and were demanding that his friends surrender the whisky jug to them. The friends were neither husky nor fighters; but it didn't take Mike Donnelly long to convince the newcomers that he would be eager to take on both of them if they wanted trouble. And he saw to it that they didn't get the whisky.

Grumbling, the strangers finally sat down on a plank near the fire, where each produced a long hunting knife and began whittling at fagot pieces, while glaring daggers at the three making merry around the jug. Some remark he heard caused one of them to ask Mike if he was headed for Lucan. Answered in the affirmative, the stranger replied: "Lucan is a good place to stay away from. They have a family of unhung thieves and murderers up there that has been raising hell for years. They're a bad bunch; they're known as the Black Donnellys!"

Mike Donnelly sprang to his feet, his Irish flaring up with his voice. "You're a liar!"

The stranger was on his feet, eyes flashing, knife held in readiness. "Take that back," he ordered, "or I'll kill you!" He began to walk forward. "Take that back or —."

"You'll kill me — kill me!" howled Mike. "Why you ugly-faced, ragged ape, I'm going to take that toad-sticker away from you and make you eat the damn thing!"

He leaped forward; the other stabbed at him with the knife. But Mike Donnelly had learned plenty, during his years as one of Biddulph's bad boys; he knew every rough-and-tumble trick in the book. His left hand caught the descending knife-arm, his knee shot up to the other's groin. The man sank to the floor with an agonized groan, to receive a deluge of Donnelly boots on his head and face. It was negligence that cost Mike his life; he forgot his opponent's pal. That individual, seeing his chum being manhandled and kicked into unconsciousness, sneaked up behind and buried his hunting knife to the hilt in Mike Donnelly's back.

Mike shouted a curse, wheeled and struck the one blow that stretched his second foe on the ground, before his own strength left him. He coughed, grasped at the air, sank to his knees then slumped forward on his face.

Mike's two friends ran for help. The evil pair got to their feet and dashed away; but they were caught within hours and eventually sentenced to long prison terms. The law found and opened a small satchel that contained Mike's Christmas gifts for the family — a pair of socks for each of his brothers, a pipe for his father and a blue cake plate, ornately wrapped in tinsel and the paper on which was written: "To Mother from Michael. Merry Xmas."

And so Mike Donnelly came home; only he came home three days after Christmas and he came in a rough-box. He was buried in the family plot, beside his brother James Jr. Father Connolly, the parish priest, preached the funeral sermon.

"I do solemnly swear, before Almighty God and his holy evangelists, never to divulge the business that may be discussed or transacted by the Biddulph Vigilance Committee, and in case I should be arrested or captured for taking part in said business, I hereby declare I will never reveal the names of my associates, even though I should be tortured or sent to the gallows for refusing to do so."

The above is the actual oath, as reported by the press, taken by the vigilantes that massacred the Donnellys.

Seemingly, with the exception of the Donnellys, there was hardly an inhabitant throughout Biddulph, by the beginning of the New Year — 1880 — who did not know that the recently elected constable, James Carroll, had organized a vigilance committee of no less than a hundred and fifty men that held regular meetings at the Swamp Schoolhouse. Just all that was discussed and planned at those meetings was not made public, of course, but it was generally opined that none of it boded good for the bad boys of Biddulph.

"Carroll is going to get rid of the Black Donnellys like he promised he would!" Those words were being whispered throughout Biddulph as the year 1880 bowed itself in.

Again tension was in the air; that terrible tension before the storm. Even the temporary respite in hostilities could not change it. There was no turning back, the inhabitants of Biddulph had suffered too much to forget the past; the Donnellys had gone too far. Lucan became as the rumbling volcano — ominous — threatening — with chaos in the offing.

Eventually, even the Donnellys became aware that something was amiss. This is evident by the words Tom Donnelly spoke to a Lucanite, less than a week before the massacre: "There is something in the wind; there is something wrong, somewhere. I feel it in my bones and so do my brothers. There is too damn much planning. Whenever we go to the village, men gather together, whisper among themselves and stare at us. Always whispering and staring at us, as though getting ready for something. Mark my words, there is hellry of some kind afoot!"

"What are you going to do about it?" the man wanted to know.

"Whatever it is, there is nothing we can do about it till it happens," was Tom's answer. "But when it does, we'll do plenty!" Unknown to Tom Donnelly, the very one he spoke to was a member of the vigilance committee.

Then on the night of January 15, 1880, and what was destined to be for the last time, the terrible Donnellys rode again while once more the skies of Biddulph flamed an angry red.

Among the men who had raided the Donnelly farmhouse was Pat "Grouchy" Ryder, who had lived on an adjoining farm for almost a quarter of a century. Once a friend, Jim and Johannah recognized the neighbor who, over a period of years, had become one of their foremost enemies. And the old couple were never one to let a wrong — when they were on the receiving end of said wrong — go either forgotten or unpunished. Pat Ryder would have to be put in his place; shown the error of his ways.

Of course by then the original fighting strength of the Donnellys had greatly diminished. Age and rheumatism had incapacitated old Jim to such an extent that he was barely able to get around; both Mike and James Jr. were now dead and Robert still in jail. However, there still remained sons Tom, William, Pat and John, a fearless and fearsome foursome when united.

According to Pat Ryder, around 11:30 on the night of January 15 just outside his farmhouse, five of the Donnellys paused in the deep snow — they had left their horses on the road — and had a loud dispute. Ryder, in his upstairs bedroom, had heard the approach of the horses, gone to the window and recognized old Jim, Johannah, Tom, William and John Donnelly. In a voice that could be heard a quarter of a mile away, in the stillness of the night, he heard Tom Donnelly shout:

"Let me go into the house and drag out that damn 'Grouchy'! I want to put him in the barn and burn it down over his head! I want to hear him sizzle and scream!"

The others were not averse to the suggestion, but they were wary of murder. Old Jim and William had served enough time to make them fairly prison shy. They compromised by burning down the barn and all the out buildings. They applauded as the flames got underway. Then shouting defiance, they mounted their horses and raced home.

Pat Ryder, barricaded inside the house, had heard and seen everything. But he made no attempt to save his property; he was in a complete panic. No sooner had the yells of the departing Donnellys faded into the distance, when Ryder was out of the house and fleeing to the security of Lucan. He was out to raise an army that would destroy the Donnellys, once and for all.

But while it is one thing to incite a mob on a hot summer night, it is quite another to coax reluctant, sleepy men out of warm beds in the middle of a bitter January night. Ryder did get his brothers, James and Thomas Ryder out of bed, and they succeeded in arousing a few more. There was talk of another raid, right then and there, on the Donnelly farmhouse, but nothing came of it. On the following morning, however, old Jim and Johannah were arrested, charged with arson, brought before a neighboring magistrate and a date set for their trial.

All Biddulph looked on with tense interest. Surely, now, there was enough "to put the old man and woman behind bars for a spell."

But there wasn't. When they were taken to trial, Pat "Grouchy" Ryder was unable to prove their guilt; it was his word against theirs. Lacking definite proof, the case was adjourned several times and at last scheduled to come up for its final disposition at the Granton court, on the morning of February 4. But what made it all so downright damnable to the surrounding countryside, was the almost certainty that the charge against Jim Donnelly and his wife would be dropped. Again they would have the last laugh. Even Constable James Carroll glumly admitted that to his vigilantes.

That did it! And how that did it! The rumbling volcano that had so long been Lucan, suddenly reached the breaking point and ceased to merely rumble and threaten. It blew its top, around 1:15 on the morning of February 4, 1880, to wallow in blood!

At this point in our story, mention of a "scoop" seems to be in order.

The writer first heard of the Donnelly feud — bits of it, at least — when traveling around the Lucan area. Twenty at the time, the history of Lucan and its violences of bygone years did not interest him. A pair of blue eyes, in the nearby village of Exeter, did. Eventually marrying the owner of the eyes, and as time went on, learning more of the feud, it became apparent at last, however, that mere hearsay, a thorough knowledge of the Lucan district or even the tales of its oldtimers, would not be enough to write the true story of the Donnellys. Seemingly endless hours of research were and did become necessary — the reading of old files, old newspapers, police and court records, etc.

But there was that one story that apparently could not be learned anywhere. Just exactly what all did happen during that massacre?

Old records tell little of that, and for the very good reason that little was ever learned of it, other than the words told by a frightened eleven-year-old boy, who was hidden under a bed while the massacre was in progress. Of course nothing was learned from the six men who were put on trial, accused of being the ringleaders of the mob that killed the Donnellys. They all denied having anything to do with the murders.

But someone must have; there can be no doubt about that. That being granted, what actual words were spoken during those terrible minutes; how were they spoken, who were they spoken to and by whom? Who began the hostilities and under what circumstances? Who struck the first blow, who killed who and all that?

There seemed to be no way of getting answers to the above questions.

Today, most of the inhabitants of the Lucan district regard the Donnelly affair as a forbidden subject, a book to be closed and forgotten. One too closely connected with family ties. After all, nearly everybody in Biddulph was connected one way or another in the downfall of the Donnellys. True, there are a few up that way who will speak of the generally known aspects of the feud; yet apparently no one wished to tell of anything that would involve themselves or the memory of their sires, with the Donnelly murders.

But persistence is a great destroyer of resistance; ten years of it finally paid off. Yes, for a good decade the writer had planned, someday, to do a book on the Donnellys, and then came the break. An elderly Biddulph inhabitant, alive at the time of the murders and whose father had been one of the members of the mob — talked! He told the writer the story of the massacre as his father, in later years, told it to him. And he told most of it in whispers.

It was not easily gained information. It was brought around only after a two year acquaintance, several visits to the home of the narrator and the consuming of — from time to time — what must have totaled a good dozen quarts of Canadian Club. The gentleman asked only that I keep his identity a secret; a vow I have faithfully adhered to. And now, here is the story, one I believe to be absolutely true in every detail. Here is the story a man told his son of the Donnelly massacre. The story of a man *who was there!*

On the night of January 3, James Carroll, along with several other leading members of the Biddulph Vigilance Committee, decided the time had come to strike, to perpetrate "the blackest crime ever committed in the Dominion."

Shortly after sundown, word having been spread by mounted messengers, men from the surrounding districts began to arrive in Lucan to gather in its bars. Grim-faced men, there was none of the customary loud laughter and talking, but there was considerable whispering among them. Sharp, questioning glances, greeted every new

arrival. Shortly after nine o'clock that night, a cutter pulling up before one of the Lucan bars — the building still
stands — caused a considerable amount of excitement and
the whispering increased.

The three who got out of the cutter were old Jim, Tom
and John Donnelly, with less than five hours between them
and eternity. Their stay in the bar was brief and as usual
they stood by themselves. Each had two fast drinks, they
purchased a bottle of rye and took their departure. Several
men stood on the sidewalk before the bar. About to get
into the cutter, Tom, wearing a beaver hat, chucked a
thumb towards the men and said to his father and brother:

"See, there is some more of them whispering behind
our backs again. Just like it was in the bar, just like it has
been for days. I tell you they're up to some damn thing."
His hands curled into fists, he took a step forward and said
to the men, "I've a good mind to beat it out of you, to
find out what it's all about!"

John stepped forward. "That might be a good idea!"

But old Jim laughed, a hand going to the shoulder of
each son. "Forget those cowardly skunks. That's all they
can do, plan and whisper. They haven't the nerve to do
anything else. Come on, boys, let's go home."

The three got in the cutter and it went up the street,
sleigh bells jingling, then out into the darkness of the
country road while behind it the village lights gleamed. At
the Donnelly farmhouse, old Jim and Tom got out of the
cutter and said goodnight to John, who then drove on to
William's place, three miles away, where he was staying.
The sands of time were ever running out.

Back in Lucan, shortly after ten o'clock, men began to
drift out of the village, in small groups and pairs, timing
their departures at intervals. But few or none of them were
homeward bound. Instead they were making for the meet-

ing place of the vigilantes, the Swamp Schoolhouse, with fierce determination the winds of that bitter cold night could not cool. Most of them, well-oiled by then, carried a bottle on the hip. One rumor has it that a generous supply of drinks awaited them at the schoolhouse.

It is known that most of the members of the mob that massacred the Donnellys were roaring drunk at the time of the attack. "It gave them the needed guts and lack of conscience to do that devilish job!"

According to the writer's informant, by eleven o'clock that night and ready for anything, there were fifty-five men assembled at the Swamp Schoolhouse. They were not a prepossessing lot, most of them, brawny and bewhiskered, with big work-hardened hands and flushed, angry faces, wore the fur caps and homespuns of the Canadian pioneer farmer. There was the constant scraping of heavy boots, wet with snow, on the schoolhouse floor. The air was thick with whisky fumes.

Once they were all inside, drinks were passed around, after which James Carroll announced: "There are too many of you. Thirty men will be enough."

Carroll then named John Kennedy, Martin McLaughlin — a prosperous farmer and a recently made Justice of the Peace — and James and Thomas Ryder, along with John Purtell, as five of those he wanted to accompany him, and said lots would be drawn to determine the other twenty-five. Fifty pieces of paper, half of them blank, half of them marked with an X, were then rolled up and placed in a hat. Those drawing the X went with Carroll. The others were told to "get along home, forget you were ever here and keep your mouths shut no matter what happens!"

When they had departed, Carroll drew the others around him and last minute plans were made. They listened attentively and nodded their understanding. When one of them mentioned something of the danger of their mission, another shouted, "Damn the danger! It's time enough to salute the devil when we meet him!" It was shortly before midnight when Carroll led them from the schoolhouse.

And so it came about that around 1:15 a.m., in the bitter cold and blackness of February 4, 1880, a mob of thirty-one men, most of them armed with clubs, though several carried spades and axes, drew near the unlit Donnelly farmhouse!

True, whisky may have deprived the mob of reason but not of cunning. Their approach was that of a clever hunter stalking dangerous game. The last quarter of a mile was made in complete silence, broken by only the shuffling of feet in the snow; and while still some two hundred yards from their objective, the men left the road and neared the structure from the rear. At a gesture from Carroll, they came to a silent halt beneath the leafless branches of a snow-covered elm tree.

Twenty yards away rose the Donnelly farmhouse, a dark outline surrounded in Erebus blackness. Overhead the stars were gleaming coldly.

James Carroll turned to the others. "You all know what to do, what is expected of you?" he whispered. At their nods, "Good! Don't forget, when I shout out, come on the run and show the bastards no mercy! Remember how they have terrorized this district for years — and kill every one of them!"

He started forward, but stopped and turned. "You know, I could use another drink — a stiff one!" he informed softly. A whisky bottle was thrust forward. "Here!" came a hoarse whisper. "A good drink of this and you'll throw stones at your grandmother!" Carroll drank deeply while the others watched, then wiping his mouth he returned the bottle to its owner with the words, "By Judas, I needed that!"

And then James Carroll walked across the intervening space till he reached the kitchen door. He raised a gloved hand and sent it against the barrier in the several hard knocks that resounded so loudly in the silence of the night. A moment's stillness followed, then more heavy raps on the door. Presently the watching men saw a light go on in an upstairs room. The breathing of all of them came faster!

CHAPTER FIFTEEN

The Massacre

Donnelly was clubbed to death, as was his wife,
Tom and Bridget murdered too.
Then the house was set on fire,
And to the skies its wild flames flew.

— Old Song

There were five persons in the Donnelly farmhouse that night.

There was old Jim, Johannah and Tom, as well as Jim's niece, Bridget, a delicate and somewhat feeble-minded girl of twenty-one, who had only recently arrived from Ireland. And there was Johnny Connor, an eleven-year-old boy who happened to be spending the night beneath the Donnelly roof. Johnny, a son of one of the very few neighbors on speaking terms with the family, had agreed to look after the farm stock while the Donnellys journeyed to their trial at Granton in the morning.

It was Johnny Connor who was to be the lone survivor of the holocaust to follow. The boy later testified in court, that on the evening of February 3, he had helped Tom Donnelly feed the pigs and do other chores, and still later, after Jim's return from Lucan, how he "helped the old man take off his boots" and had gone to bed "along with him." By 11 p.m., lights were out in the house and the family slept. Of course the chief topic that night had been the scheduled court appearance of Jim and Johannah on the morrow.

Johannah was the first to be awakened by the loud knocking on the door. She aroused Bridget, lit a candle then called down to Tom, who slept in the room below. Presently, in bare feet, attired only in his long, heavy underwear and yawning, Tom Donnelly made his way to the kitchen, set the candle he carried down on the table and opened the door. Burly James Carroll, anything but handsome, stood before him.

Tom Donnelly was still yawning, little suspecting the terrible death that was to be his in a matter of minutes. He rubbed a hand over his sleepy eyes and asked casually: "Yeah? Who are you and what do you want?"

Carroll scowled at the other's indifference. He replied with a sharp, "I'm Constable James Carroll and I'm here on business!" A pause, then he asked, "Well, have I got to stand out here in the cold?"

Plainly, the listening men heard Tom's answer: "I don't give a damn what you do! You can stand out there or stand on your head if you want to!" Then he mentioned something else Carroll could do "if you want to!"

Tom Donnelly went to the table and lit several more candles. Carroll entered the kitchen, leaving the door open and winter blasts blew in. Tom wheeled. "Close the door, you half-wit!" he howled. "Where in hell were you born — in a barn?" He picked up his half-filled pipe from the table and reached for one of the candles.

Carroll closed the door, one hand in his coat pocket, and walked forward, saying, "Too bad I'm here as an officer of the law. I'd like to try for that prize offered to any man that can lick you — a year's supply of drinks. I think I could win it, Donnelly!"

"I've spit in the faces of better men than you, Carroll. If you want to fight, just say so!" He brought the lighted candle up to his pipe.

"I'd like nothing better, but that will have to wait awhile. As I said, I'm here on official business. Tom Donnelly, I've a warrant for your arrest!"

James Carroll struck with lightning speed. Tom, unafraid, sure of himself, had been lighting his pipe, his eyes upon it, his hands close together as the other spoke. He was to pay a stiff price for that unguarded moment. James Carroll's hand whipped from his pocket then both of them shot forward. There was a flash of steel, a metallic "click" — and handcuffs were on the wrists of Tom Donnelly!

In a voice oozing satisfaction, Carroll exlaimed: "There — that will hold you, my bucko!"

It was break number one for Special Constable James Carroll. His trick had worked. Granted, Carroll was a fearless man and a rough-and-tumble brawler of note; but ordinarily, this writer doubts if he could have put cuffs on Tom Donnelly in a hundred years of trying. Break number two for Carroll was the absence of Pat Donnelly that night. On the previous day Pat had gone over to the village of Thorold, and was not expected back for several days.

As Carroll concluded his remark, Johannah and Bridget, in long-sleeved and high-necked flannelette nightgowns, appeared in the doorway between the kitchen and the front room. Each held a candle and Johannah demanded, "What's going on here?"

Carroll answered, "Enforcing a bit of law and high time it was done. Where is your husband?" Johannah nodded to the nearby bedroom and asked Carroll why he wanted him. "To tell him he's under arrest!" was the constable's reply. He took the candle from Bridget's hand, brushed the two women aside and made his way to the bedroom. In the kitchen, Tom Donnelly was staring at the handcuffs on his wrists in a dazed manner. "What the hell," he kept repeating. "What the hell."

By then old Jim Donnelly, sleeping with the Connor boy, had been roused. Slipping into his pants, he met Carroll head-on in the bedroom doorway. Another quick movement on the constable's part, and handcuffs snapped around the old man's wrists as he heard: "You're under arrest, James Donnelly!"

It seems almost a certainty that James Carroll did not notice Johnny Connor who, awakened, was sitting upright in bed and staring at the two men, his young eyes wide.

With James Donnelly ahead of him, Carroll returned to the kitchen. Johannah and Bridget now stood near Tom. Old Jim's eyes fell on the cuffs on his son's wrists. "What, Tom, has he got handcuffs on you, too?" From the bedroom, Johnny Connor heard Tom's answer: "Yes, the sneaky bastard! He slipped them on while I was lighting my pipe. He thinks he's smart!"

"Oh, Tom!" wailed Johannah.

"Don't worry, mother, you've nothing to fear from the skunk. Even with these handcuffs on, I can beat him to the floor and take the key from him."

"Let's find out what all this is about," old Jim spoke up. "You say we are under arrest, Carroll. Alright, then, read the warrant." But Carroll answered, "Later, later."

"Do it now!" ordered Tom. "If you have a warrant, we've a right to hear it and you know it!"

But again Carroll's reply was the evasive, "Later, later."

For a brief silence the others stared at him, then Tom Donnelly turned to his father. "I don't like this; something's wrong here. He says he has a warrant for our arrest, and he won't read it. I'll tell you what; I don't think he has a warrant." He turned to the constable. "Just what the hell are you up to, Carroll?"

And then Johannah seemed to sense it, to know that some terrible danger was near at hand. "It's a trap!" she cried. "A trap! The lying devil has tricked you, has you both in handcuffs and is ready to kill all of us! Do something quick or..."

She got no farther. James Carroll leaped to the door, flung it open and shouted into the darkness: "Come on, out there — hurry! I've got them handcuffed! Come and give it to them! Hurry — hurry!"

The next moment a mob of hostile, shouting men, came pouring through the doorway. The time was approximately 1:23 a.m.

John Kennedy, the brother-in-law of William Donnelly and howling like a madman, was the first member of the mob that bounded into the kitchen. Behind him came the others. Kennedy carried two clubs, and as prearranged, tossed one to James Carroll, who caught it, wheeled — and made straight for Johannah Donnelly, yelling: "You've had this comin' to you for years, you old she-devil!"

Tom Donnelly did not wait for the deluge to come to him. He sprang forward to meet the men, chopping his manacled wrists like sledges. His first blow broke the jaw of a member of the mob, rendering the man hors de combat.

As the men came surging through the doorway, old Jim seized a kitchen chair with his handcuffed hands and gave the Donnelly glare. Most of them shouting, drunk and unkempt, it was a wild-looking horde he faced. But for all his three score and then some years, Jim Donnelly gave a good account of himself in his final moments. As though suddenly possessed with the strength of his youth, he fought as a veritable demon, dying with the same disregard for fear that he had shown throughout his long life.

Nor did that last stand reveal any yellow in the make-up of Johannah. As James Carroll came towards her with uplifted club, the old gal from the Galty Mountains, defiant to the last, had already grasped a flatiron from the top of the stove. She heaved it at Carroll's head as she cursed him.

The young girl, Bridget, screamed, then turned and ran into the darkness of the front room. John Purtell, the half-baked farmhand and drunk as a loon, ran after her with the axe he carried. His feet got in his own way and he fell flat on his face; but finally getting up, he reeled after her, yelling, "I'll bash the young sow's head in!"

Kill-crazed men, shouting and cursing, continued to come through the doorway, while the clubs of the first attackers were put into use, rising and falling. The pent-up hatred of years was being loosened in those wild moments!

The kitchen literally packed with struggling humanity, old Jim, forced against a far wall, fought on till the chair, his only weapon, was splintered to pieces on the heads of his enemies. But this had been a vicious as well as gallant last stand, and when he finally went down he had three men beneath him. Yet his efforts aroused neither praise nor pity. The mob beat him to pulp. Then one of the men came forward with an axe and chopped off Jim Donnelly's head. Thus perished the father of the bad boys of Biddulph.

The mob made no concession to Johannah's sex; she perished, horribly, near her spouse. The flatiron she threw at Carroll went wide and crashed through a window, but old Johannah, biting and clawing, fought like a mad thing. As the men swarmed around her and their clubs rose and fell, she cursed them with her final breath. Struggling to reach her husband, shouting, "May you all roast in hell!" she was beaten to her knees, then to an outstretched position, face downward on the floor, her long, gray hair a gory mass with strands of it clinging to the bludgeons of the mob. They continued to club her long after she ceased to live.

Bridget Donnelly, running into the semi-darkness of the front room, with drunken John Purtell, axe raised, staggering after her, sought to reach and escape from the house through one of the front windows.

But the attack on the Donnellys had been thoroughly planned; not all of the mobsters had gone inside the house. Besides those in the kitchen, there were four other downstairs' windows in the house, which together with the front door offered five exits of escape for the Donnellys. Ten of the thirty men staying outside the house, two of them stationed themselves before each exit with ready clubs. Plainly they could hear the terrible din that came from within and knew what it signified.

Then a young girl, face white with terror, suddenly appeared before one of the windows and flung it open. It was Bridget Donnelly, fleeing from the clumsy Purtell and far enough ahead of him to make good her dash for freedom. But she threw up the window only to stare at the faces of the two men on guard before it. They sprang towards her, lashing out with their clubs.

With that wail of despair that announced her last hope had vanished, Bridget Donnelly turned, dodged around the oncoming Purtell and running to the stairway, hurried up it to her bedroom. But several of the men were right behind her. She was caught in the bedroom, knocked to the floor, seized by the heels and dragged down the stairs — her head bumping on the steps, her screams ringing out. She was clubbed to death at the foot of the stairway, amid loud and terrible laughter, by several members of the mob.

Tom was the last of the Donnellys to go down. And for awhile it looked as though he just wasn't going to go down. He showed why the prize offered to any man who could lick him was never claimed.

Chopping bone-breaking blows with his manacled hands, he ploughed straight into the mob — took the offensive. His fast movements, weaving and dodging, made him an almost impossible target for the clubs of his foes. Eventually forced back to the wall, with a wild blaze of fury and a loud Donnelly war cry, he once more took the offensive, slashed and slugged his way across the kitchen, reached the door and struggled through it in the furious outburst that put most of the mob behind him. He was breaking into the clear when a thrown pitchfork sank deep into his back.

Tom Donnelly was dragged back into the kitchen, through it and to the front room, where the men went to work on him. Two minutes later he was like nothing human, ripped, slashed and beaten apart. Then his head was chopped off. Johnny Connor chose about that time to peek from the bedroom, and later told in court that the men, "were doing something terrible to Tom."

After that one brief glimpse, Johnny did what might be expected, under the circumstances, of any eleven-year-old boy. He ran back into the bedroom and hid under the bed.

To the best of their knowledge, the entire household annihilated, the men then proceeded to burn down the house. Coal oil was sprinkled heavily in all the rooms, then ignited and the Donnelly farmhouse became a blazing crematorium, in the midst of a mad, inhuman howling from the mob. So once again and for the last time of its almost thirty-three years duration, the Donnelly feud caused waves of flame to light the Lucan skies, while James Carroll shouted: "Come, men, we must not idle here. This night's work is only half-done!"

Johnny Connor testified in court:

"After they murdered the old man, the old woman, Bridget and Tom, the men poured coal oil all over the house. They came into the room where I was hiding and poured coal oil on the bed I was under. Then they all ran out when they set fire to it, and I got from under the bed, put on my pants and tried to quench the fire with my coat. I went to the front room and saw Tom dead on the floor. I went to the kitchen and tramped upon the old woman. There was a light from the fire in the room where I was sleeping, from the kitchen and also from Tom's bedroom. I got out of the house and I could see the mob walking up the road.

"I ran over to Pat Whelan's place."

" 'Let's get the rest,' cried Carroll.
'We want every Donnelly dead!'
They hurried to a nearby house,
And blew off John Donnelly's head."

— Old Song

Meanwhile the mob was advancing upon the home of William Donnelly, with the threat: "That devil of a cripple gets it next!"

The mob did not have its former strength, however. The man whose jaw Tom Donnelly had broken, and two more who had come in contact with his hard fists, along with another whose sconce had been slightly warped by the chair old Jim wielded, fell out and made for their homes. Those four marked desertion number one.

The walk to William's house was long, the hour pitch-black; the cold would have made a Spartan sob!

For many of the mob the murder lust was fast wearing off. The terrible cold may have accounted for part of it, but there was that other outstanding factor — the whisky had given out. With every forward step, enthusiasm waned. Then singly and in pairs, the men began to fall out, despite the urgings and oratory of Carroll and John Kennedy. But even their hot words could not heat the atmosphere nor supply the juice that cheers. By the time the house of William Donnelly loomed up in the darkness, only eight men walked behind Kennedy and Carroll, and all of them were faltering badly.

It was now going on to 3 a.m.

In front of the gateway, the men drew together. Two of them carried shotguns but hadn't the heart to use them. Their reluctance angered Carroll. He finally tore the guns from their hands, called them yellow-livered skunks, and handed one of the guns to Kennedy, saying: "Here, John, I know I can depend on you." Kennedy answered grimly: "You sure can, Jim. I've dreamed of killing that club-footed devil for years!"

James Ryder spoke up in a hesitant, uncertain manner. "I — I guess I can go with — with you two, but I haven't any gun." Carroll demanded, "You have a club, haven't you?" Ryder nodded and agreed to go with them.

So the three men quietly entered the gateway and stole towards the house, while the others gave half-hearted support from the roadway. They heard Carroll say to Kennedy, "We'll make this one fast!" Then once again silence was desecrated by the loud banging on a door.

Three people were in the house. John Donnelly occupied a small room near the front door, while William and his wife slept in an adjoining bedroom. The knocking on the door woke both John and the wife of William, but she had to shake and awaken her sleeping husband. William, still digging fists into sleepy eyes, was just getting out of his bed when his brother answered the door. John Donnelly never had a chance, either to defend himself or even as much as to recognize his killers. As he swung the door open, two shotguns roared out.

Riddled with more than thirty slugs, one loud groan escaped him. He took two steps forward, then at the edge of the low porch, crying, "I'm hit — hit!" John Donnelly plunged face down into the snow, dead almost instantly!

His killers had not waited to see him die. The instant their guns had gone off, Carroll and Kennedy, along with James Ryder, turned and ran back to the others on the road. Even then, it is evident, they were under the impression they had killed William, for as they ran through the gateway, Carroll called out to the others: "The clubfooted devil is dead! We've done for him!"

They dashed off into the darkness, seeking only to conceal themselves. They did not see William Donnelly come to the doorway then hurry to and bend over his dead brother.

Two miles from the home of William, James Carroll and the nine others, half-frozen, stopped at the home of one of the mobsters who had left them earlier. They told the man of the latest murder, naming William Donnelly as the victim. There they had several drinks of whisky and warmed themselves. And there each took the hand of the other and swore on the family Bible, to remain silent and deny they had, or knew anyone that had, anything to do with the Biddulph murders. The first streaks of gray were beginning to lighten the eastern skies when the men left the farmhouse, each going his respective way to his own home.

And that is the story of the Donnelly massacre, as told to the writer by a man who heard it from his own father — a father who was one of the mobsters!

CHAPTER SIXTEEN

The Sunset of The Donnellys

Six ringleaders were put on trial,
But they were all set free.
It was said men deserve medals,
Who will kill a Black Donnelly.

— Old Song

The following morning, Thursday, February 5, 1880, and splashed over half of page one, Toronto's The Globe carried the following — the first of a series of stories on "The Biddulph Tragedy" that was to last for months:

HORRIBLE TRAGEDY AT LUCAN
Five Persons Murdered By Mob

An Entire Household Sacrificed

Result Of A Family Feud

30 Men Engaged In The Bloody Work

The Story As Told By A Child Witness Of The Crime

LUCAN, Feb. 4 — Lucan awoke this morning to shock the country with intelligence of the blackest crime ever committed in the Dominion.

The crime consisted of the murder, or rather butchery, of a family of five — father, mother, two brothers, and a girl. The victims were named Donnelly, a family that has lived in the neighborhood for upwards of thirty years. They resided on Lot 18, 6th Concession of Biddulph. The farm consists of fifty acres. They bore the unenviable reputation of being:

"The terrors of the township!"

With the Donnelly house in flames behind him, the boy Johnny Connor, had run over to the farmhouse of Pat Whelan and told his harrowing tale. But such was the reign of terror in the district, that no member of the Whelan household would venture forth. It was not until around 11 a.m. that morning when the crime was investigated by County Constable Alfred Brown. By then, of course, the Donnelly house was completely demolished, the bodies of the dead were horribly charred.

Acting on the information supplied by Johnny Connor, James Carroll was the first member of the mob to be arrested. Other arrests followed. In all, fourteen members of the vigilance committee were brought in; men who had been seen and recognized by young Connor. The accused were arraigned on the charge of murder in the police court in London, on February 21, 1880.

While the police court investigation was proceeding in London, a coroner's inquest was held in Lucan, the verdict of the jury being that "James Donnelly, Johannah Donnelly, Bridget Donnelly and Thomas Donnelly came to their death by being murdered and burned by parties unknown." Also, that John Donnelly came to his death "by gunshot wounds at the hands of a party or parties unknown to the jury."

It was evident that no jury could be found in Lucan who would bring in a verdict against those who had committed the massacre. And a popular expression around Lucan was: "Any jury that would hang the men who killed the Donnellys, ought to be hung themselves."

In London, the police court magistrate discharged a number of those arrested, and finally committed for trial on the charge of murder, James Carroll, John Kennedy, Martin McLaughlin, John Purtell and James and Thomas Ryder. Accused of being the ringleaders of the mob that massacred the Donnellys, the six came up for trail at the Spring Assizes in London, on April 12, 1880, before Mr. Justice Wilson.

Aemilius — afterwards Sir Aemilius — Irvin, represented the prosecution and immediately moved for a change of venue to some other county, on the grounds that the prevailing state of public feeling would not permit a fair trail. This was denied but a postponement of the trial was ordered. The six prisoners, consequently, did not come up for trail until the Autumn Assizes at London, in October.

Long before then, of course, the murdered Donnellys had been buried. Father Connolly, the parish priest, conducted the burial services. On numerous occasions in the past, it was said that the good man, always without success, had pleaded with Jim Donnelly and his sons to mend their ways.

Time for the trial, it was decided that the prisoners should be tried separately, and James Carroll was the first to be put in the dock, charged with the murder of Johannah Donnelly. Johnny Connor repeated his story, and though cross-examined for more than three hours, never once contradicted himself. On the major points of his evidence he was most emphatic.

"Who was the man you say went into the bedroom of James Donnelly?" asked the defence.

"James Carroll," said Johnny.

"You could be mistaken, couldn't you?"

"I'm not mistaken; my eyes are good," was the boy's answer.

However, the jury failed to agree and a new trial was ordered. Meanwhile, most of the inhabitants of Biddulph were firm as to their opinions, all of which favored the six men accused of being the ringleaders of the mob. One Lucanite told a reporter of the London Advertiser: "Every one around here will agree with me, when I say that the men that killed the Donnellys should all be given medals of solid gold, and special seats in heaven!"

The second trial took place in the last week in January 1881, with the defence of James Carroll being conducted by three outstanding Canadian lawyers. The trial came to an end on February 2, at 2:55 p.m., when the jury filed back into the courtroom and foreman Francis arose and announced: "Not guilty!"

Cheers rang out in the courtroom!

With the acquittal of James Carroll the charges against the other five were dropped, since the evidence against him was identical with that against them.

James Carroll, along with Martin McLaughlin, John Kennedy, John Purtell and James and Thomas Ryder, returned to Lucan in triumph and were greeted in the manner of homecoming heroes. The town band met them and blared sour notes, while the mayor gave a speech of welcome and the populace struggled to shake their hands. A reception was held in their honor at the Central Hotel, and later that night a dance was given. Joy and festivities hitherto unknown, reigned in Lucan. The six were acclaimed as being: "The redeemers of the community!"

It was while the dance was at its height, with music and laughter coming from the brilliantly lit Central Hotel, that a tall, well-built man, prison-pallor on his handsome face, walked up the main street of Lucan and entered the Western Bar. It was Robert Donnelly, having completed his sentence in the penitentiary, returning to his home village.

There were twelve or so men in the Western Bar at the time, most of them commenting on the festivities in the hotel across the street, when Robert Donnelly entered. Their gazes went to the door as it swung open, a few gasps arose then came an immediate silence. The blue eyes of Robert Donnelly were icy cold. Slowly his gaze went from one to the other. It was a safe bet that at least several of them had been a member of the mob that slaughtered his parents and brothers. And it is equally certain that he realized the fact. Standing in the doorway, watching them, that sudden silence continued for a long minute.

Then Robert Donnelly made that last Donnelly attempt at authority in Lucan. He walked over to the bar, flung a five dollar bill upon it and turned to the men, one hand gesturing to the hotel across the street. "They're having a hell of a good time over there, celebrating the butchery of my people and kissing the hands of the killers. Well, suppose we have a little celebrating here!"

Then his eyes narrowed, once more was seen "the Donnelly glare" and he commanded: "Now I want all of you damn murderers to step up to the bar and have a drink on me!"

It was no go; it was a complete failure. Times had changed in the old town during his years in prison. For several seconds the men stared at him, then one of them laughed and said, "Go to hell!"

That broke the spell. The next moment they were all laughing at him, loud guffaws of derision and mockery that rang out to tell they regarded any orders or commands on his part as little more than a joke. Robert Donnelly finally walked out of the bar, got on his horse and rode up the street, while music still came from the Central Hotel and jeering laughter resounded in the Western Bar behind him. It told all. Fear of Biddulph's bad boys had gone — vamoosed — vanished. From now on their presence would arouse only mockery or pity. They were washed up! All through!

It was the sunset of the Donnellys!

There is little else to be told of the Donnelly feud.

Discouraged, their spirits broken and time beginning to dust their hair, the three remaining brothers moved elsewhere, with no attempts made at retaliation. Robert Donnelly held several positions in various parts of Ontario following his release from prison, and for some years before his death was a night clerk in a London hotel. William Donnelly moved from the Lucan area, though he and his wife were later returned to and buried in the family plot. Oddly enough, during the years that followed the massacre, Patrick Donnelly, who in his younger days had been the most stable of the boys, began an erratic and seemingly tireless wandering over the width and breadth of Canada. He died in 1929.

The story is still told of Patrick Donnelly's eccentricity. As the years passed the massacre of his parents and brothers preyed more heavily on his mind, and he seemed to live for only one purpose — to attend the funerals of the six men who had been accused of being the ringleaders of the mob and were later released.

And it was his luck to outlive all of them.

No matter where he was, he made it a point to learn of each death and attend the burial. At every funeral he could be observed in the Lucan graveyard, like some macabre scarecrow. He would stand quietly in the background, saying nothing, while relatives wept and brief prayers were uttered. Then, as the coffin was being lowered into the ground, Patrick Donnelly would leap forward, spit upon it, raise his eyes and clenched fist to the skies with a scream of incredibly wild triumph, and shout out:

"There goes another of the bastards to hell!"

"Oh all young folks take warning,
Never live a life of hate,
Of wickedness or violence, lest
You share the Donnelly's fate.
Their murdered bodies lie today,
A mile from Lucan town.
But the memories of the awful feud,
Time never will live down!"

— *Old Song*

THE END